KT-431-771

The Second Reformation

The Second Reformation

Reshaping the Church for the
Twenty-First Century

William A. Beckham

TOUCH Publications
P.O. Box 19888
Houston, TX 77224

Copyright © 1995, 1996, 1997 by William A. Beckham.
Published by TOUCH Publications

All rights reserved. No part of this publication may be reproduced, stored in a retrieval system, or transmitted in any form or by any means, electronic, mechanical, photocopy, recording or otherwise, without the prior written consent of the publisher.

International Standard Book Number: 1-880828-90-1

All Scripture quotations, unless otherwise indicated, are from the New American Standard Bible, copyrighted 1960, 1962, 1963, 1968, 1971, 1972, 1973, 1975, 1977, 1987, 1988, The Lockman Foundation. Used by permission.

Scripture quotations marked NIV are from the New International Version, Copyright 1973, 1978, 1984 by International Bible Society. Used by permission.

Editing, book layout, cover design and illustration: Scott Boren, Joey Beckham, Peter Sukoneck, and Jennifer Gressett.

TOUCH Publications is the book-publishing division of TOUCH Outreach Ministries, a resource and consulting ministry for churches with a vision for cell-based local church structure.

FOR A FREE CATALOG OF
TOUCH PUBLICATIONS BOOKS AND MATERIALS,
PLEASE CALL
1-800-735-5865 (USA)
281-497-7901 (INTERNATIONAL)
281-497-0904 (FAX)

DEDICATION

To the theologians, philosophers and prophets of God's Second Reformation and twenty-first century revolution. Their writings and creative thinking are the foundation of my church pilgrimage. Representatives of this group are:

Dietrich Bonhoeffer, who even in prison still lived *life together* in community. **Elton Trueblood**, apostle to the *company of the committed* community. **Robert Coleman**, who showed us the *master plan* of New Testament leadership. **Francis Schaeffer**, who led the church's *escape from reason*. **Ray Stedman**, who taught us the meaning of *body life*. **Howard A. Snyder**, who describes both the old and new *kingdom wineskin*. **David (formerly Paul) Yonggi Cho**, who has taught us about *successful home cell groups*. **Ralph W. Neighbour Jr.**, a prophetic voice showing *where we go from here*.

The modern cell church movement is the fruit of their faithfulness to the vision of the church God placed in their hearts.

CONTENTS

LIST OF FIGURES

FOREWORD

J esus is the Savior of the world. Is He also the Lord of the church? Do we really believe it? Hebrews 11:10 says that God is the master "architect and builder." The church often neglects or ignores the basic design revealed to us in Scripture. We praise the Head but fail to build the body.

Most of our church traditions are either *presbyterian, episcopal or congregational* in form. That is, they focus on the importance of presbyters or elders, on qualified overseers and pastors, or on the local community of believers. Each of these emphases traces back to the New Testament; each preserves a biblical insight. But none fully embodies the biblical dynamic of the church. Whatever our view of church polity, the more basic question today is: Are our churches really incarnating the Gospel of Jesus Christ? Have we paid enough attention to the basic biblical ecclesiology, whatever our particular traditions? Significantly, writers from across the ecclesiastical spectrum have been calling for a new reformation. And often they come to similar conclusions about the organic, cellular nature of the church when they examine the New Testament material.

I have heard calls for a New Reformation in the church for more than twenty years—one that would renew the church's form and corporate life, making it both faithful and effective. And God has been at work over these years. *The Second Reformation* is a sign of this. More than another call for church renewal, this book points the way forward—especially with regard to the organic, cellular nature of Christ's Body.

Drawing on extensive experience as missionary, church planter, pastor, and teacher, Bill Beckham combines biblical insights, historical and theological analysis, and practical common sense in this important book. He joins the growing chorus of concerned leaders who are calling God's people back to the biblical model—precisely in order to be faithfully effective in this day of emerging global society. *The Second Reformation* is an informed, sustained argument for the New Testament pattern of large-group celebration wed to small-group discipleship.

We can learn much from history. My own research has convinced me that whenever God renews the church, key elements are a *rediscovery of close-knit community and the ministry of all believers.* As Beckham reminds us, the "Two-Winged Church" is really not new. We have instructive examples from history. We simply need to discover again what the church, at some level, has always known.

The Second Reformation is a call to biblical faithfulness in the way we form our life together as a Christian church. It is a reminder of the kind of shared life we are called to as Christians, and a practical guide on how to incarnate the awesome Good News of Jesus Christ in this critical turn-of-millennium age. The book sparkles with insights and examples. It shows us what it would mean to genuinely "cell-ebrate" the church.

—Howard A. Snyder, author of *The Problem of Wineskins, Signs of the Spirit: How God Reshapes the Church,* and *EarthCurrents: The Struggle for the World's Soul*

INTRODUCTION

EZEKIEL'S BIG PICTURE

*The hand of the Lord was upon me, and He brought
me out by the Spirit of the Lord and set me down in
the middle of the valley; and it was full of bones.
And He caused me to pass among them round about,
and behold, there were very many on the surface of
the valley: and lo, they were very dry.*
—Ezekiel 37:1-2

The prophet Ezekiel's vision of the valley of dry bones expresses frustration, yet ultimately hope, with the nation of Israel. As Ezekiel looked over the valley, clearly he did not lack for bones. Plenty of bones and parts were scattered over the valley surface. But "can these bones live?" Where was the form, flesh, and life around the bones?

God instructed Ezekiel to prophesy over the bones. "And as I prophesied, there was a noise and behold, a rattling; and the bones came together, bone to its bone. And I looked, and behold, sinews were on them; and flesh grew, and skin covered them" (Ezekiel 37:7-8). All of the parts became connected and integrated into a whole. But this was still not enough: "There was no breath in them. . . . Prophesy to the breath."

Form without the breath of God is still nothing more than connected dry bones. "So I prophesied as He commanded me, and the breath came into them, and they came to life, and stood on their feet, an exceedingly great army" (Ezekiel 37:10). Dry, dead, disconnected bones were transformed into a mighty, living army.

A MACRO VIEW

This book is part of the dialogue about the New Testament church as it relates to the world of the twenty-first century. I write not because I am an expert, but because, like you, I have carried the vision of the New Testament church in my heart for decades. Like Ezekiel, I have stood on the valley floor surveying the dry bones of the church and longed for the power to prophesy form and life into it. I now suspect the old approach of "doing church" used for seventeen hundred years will never cause much more than a "rattling of the bones." Like Israel, the church lacks a spiritual system to unite it into an organism which God can fill with His breath.

By design this book is a *macro* look at the church. Macro means combining form in a perspective that is "long, large, enlarged." A common proverb that expresses the macro versus micro principle is "you can't see the forest for the trees." We often can't "see the forest" (macro) "for the trees" (micro). We get lost in the details and fail to see the big picture.

To some, this approach will prove frustrating because details, specifics, methods and materials are usually seen as the keys to success. However, from my own experience, as a pastor and missionary, my problem in implementing strategy is usually not a *micro*—or a detail problem—but a *macro,* a big picture problem. Once I understand the large picture, I can fit the details in their proper place.

A PUZZLE WITHOUT THE PICTURE

As church leaders, it seems we stand before a box containing a 5000 piece puzzle, but don't know what the puzzle looks like. The pieces are obviously designed to fit together. However, the big picture necessary to arrange the pieces is missing. I can imagine Ezekiel having the same thoughts as he surveyed the dry bones in the valley.

This sense of uncertainty often occurs during periods of rapid change, when accepted patterns of operation have failed, yet new ones have not filled the void. Copernicus lived in such a transitional time. He described the chaotic state of astronomy in his day: ". . . it is as though an artist were to gather the hands, feet, head and other members for his images from diverse models, each part excellently drawn, but not related to a single body, and since they in no way match each other, the result would be monster rather than man."[1]

Ezekiel, Copernicus, and church leaders today all share a common problem—we lack a framework that integrates our system. Standing before the puzzle of the church, we have more parts than we can manage. And it will do little good to once again shake all the pieces up in the box to give them a different look! We must first fit the methods and details into a macro vision of the New Testament church.

A MACRO VIEW CAN BE SCARY

Visualizing the church in new, broad strokes can prove frightening because it takes us above our comfortable surroundings. We are no longer in control. The macro view of the church is as large and encompassing as God Himself, and stretches us beyond our limited time and space dimensions. It takes us far above the safety of our logical physical world into God's spiritual realm of vision and faith.

Therefore, *this book is really about you and me.* Before the church can change, you and I must change. Simply changing materials, programs, and activities is not enough. We must change how we perceive the church, how we see God expressing Himself in the world through the church, and how we do church.

LET US "PROPHESY"

Walk with me into the valley with all the bones and parts of the church we have tried to rattle and bring to life. We should be familiar with these bones. We have walked among them and stepped over them for years. We have tied them together with our programs, and we have shaken them with all of our administrative and promotional might. Yes, we know the bones well.

However, God has commanded us to *prophesy to the bones* and *prophesy to the breath.* So this time, instead of rattling the bones with our own strength, let us prophesy the words of God upon the church. Prophesy upon the bones to give form. Prophesy the breath of God so the form will come alive as God's church, a mighty living army marching into reformation—*The Second Reformation.*

PART I
WHY A SECOND REFORMATION?

Now, after more than three centuries, we can, if we will, change gears again. Our opportunity for a big step lies in opening the ministry to the ordinary Christian in much the same manner that our ancestors opened Bible reading to the ordinary Christian. To do this means, in one sense, the inauguration of a new Reformation while in another it means the logical completion of the earlier Reformation in which the implications of the position taken were neither fully understood nor loyally followed.
—Elton Trueblood

1
UNCLOGGING THE DRAIN

The thinking which created the problems
we have today is insufficient to solve them.
—Albert Einstein

Christian Smith's tub was clogged for three days. He assumed it was the result of some recent remodeling. He spent the better part of three days trying to fix it and even went to the basement to attack the drain with a "plumbing snake" from below.

Nothing worked. There wasn't even a trickle of water. He finally gave up. Exhausted, defeated and covered with twenty-year-old drain muck, he sat on the edge of the tub and considered life without a shower. He goes on to explain, "Suddenly, I had a sinking feeling. It couldn't be. I reached over to the drain toggle and flicked it up. Instantly, the dirty water swooshed down the drain in a liquid twister. I had left the drain plug down."[1]

Christian Smith applied his clogged drain experience to the church:

The obvious moral of my drain debacle was this: no solution, no matter how creative or high-powered, can succeed if you have defined the problem incorrectly. Put differently: more important than giving the right answers is asking the right questions. And differently again: when you prematurely limit the range of possible causes of your problems, you are likely to end up with drain muck in your face.

To get my tub fixed, I needed to step back and consider whether the trouble was something other than horsehair plaster. I needed to approach my problem in a totally different frame of mind, with a radically reordered interpretation of the evidence. Likewise, to get the church fixed, we also need to step back, set aside the conventional assumptions about what's wrong, and approach the problem with a radically different frame of reference.[2]

Our frames of reference, or *paradigms,* shape how we view and what we think about the events around us. We interpret our experiences and our relationships with people, events and structures through our paradigms. We also cannot understand the church unless we see the church within its *New Testament paradigm.* This chapter defines and illustrates paradigm thinking and shows its relevancy to what is happening in the church today. How we *do* church is directly related to how we *think* church.

PARADIGM PICTURES

In his book *The Structure of Scientific Revolution,* Thomas Kuhn introduced our generation to the word *paradigm* and the phrase *paradigm shift.* He claimed every significant breakthrough in the field of science is a break with old, traditional ways of thinking. Steven Covey confirms this as he defines paradigm for us:

> The word paradigm comes from the Greek word *paradigma:* a pattern or map for understanding and explaining certain aspects of reality. While a person may make small improvements by developing new skills, quantum leaps in performance and revolutionary advances in technology require new maps, new paradigms, new ways of thinking about and seeing the world.[3]

Professor Kuhn gives examples of well known scientific discoveries which started when a scientist broke from the accepted pattern of conceptualizing a body of facts. He observed quantum leaps in creativity and advancement when scientists began to perceive a situation in a new way because of a shift in understanding. The phrase *paradigm shift* was coined to explain this extraordinary process.

Although *paradigm* was originally a scientific term, many use it today to mean a model, theory, perception, a basic underlying assumption, or a frame of reference. Today, the phrase is a buzz word in the political and business worlds. Christian leaders have also begun to apply the concept to the church.

Paradigm thinking is no modern phenomenon, as verified in the following letter from Martin Van Buren to President Andrew Jackson. Reading between the lines gives the impression that two transportation paradigms triggered a fierce debate in American politics during the early part of the nineteenth century.

January 31, 1829
Martin Van Buren
Governor of New York

To President Jackson:
The canal system of this country is being threatened by a new form of transportation known as "railroads." The federal government must preserve the canals for the following reasons:

One. If canal boats are supplanted by "railroads," serious unemployment will result. Captains, cooks, drivers, hostelers, repairmen and dock tenders will be left without means of livelihood, not to mention the numerous farmers now employed in growing hay for the horses.

Two. Boat builders would suffer and towline, whip and harness makers would be left destitute.

Three. Canal boats are absolutely essential to the defense of the United States. In the event of the expected trouble with England, the Erie Canal would be the only means by which we could ever move the supplies so vital to waging modern war.

As you may well know, Mr. President, "railroad" carriages are pulled at the enormous speed of fifteen miles per hour by "engines" which, in addition to endangering life and limb of passengers, roar and snort their way through the countryside, setting fire to crops, scaring livestock and frightening women and children. The Almighty surely never intended that people should travel at such breakneck speed.[4]

Paradigm thinking has always existed. The first person who used fire to cook his meal or carried a burden on a round wheel was a paradigm thinker. Who peeled the first banana and ate it? Whoever he was, he did it because he thought differently from all the others who had passed by that banana tree.

Recently, I saw a picture of a map used by Christopher Columbus 500 years ago to make his "discovery" of the New World. No wonder he didn't get to India! His maps were incomplete, and his conclusions were faulty. Columbus found the New World through luck or providence—his maps deserve little credit for his discoveries.

What would happen if Columbus' maps were substituted for our modern maps? How would that affect air and ship navigation? The impact would be devastating. A new base of assumptions and an incomplete framework would exist. Would you board a ship or airplane using Columbus' maps? I certainly wouldn't!

VERTICAL AND HORIZONTAL THINKING

Several decades ago, Edward DeBono introduced the concept of vertical and lateral thinking. He observed that typical thinking patterns tend to dig a hole vertically, going deeper and deeper within the accepted way of processing a certain kind of information. At the bottom of this processing "hole" are the experts who keep digging deeper and deeper into the same hole of information which they accept as the "given" for a particular subject. This is what he calls vertical thinking.

Lateral or horizontal thinking happens when an innovator gets out of the old information hole and begins to think in the light of new territory. New ways of thinking and processing information emerge because information is no longer restricted and limited only to the old context of thinking or the old process.

The purpose of thinking is to collect information and to make the best possible use of it. Because of the way the mind works to create fixed concept patterns, we cannot make the best use of new information unless we have some means for restructuring the old patterns and bringing them up to date. Our traditional methods of thinking teach us how to refine such patterns and establish their validity. But we shall always make less than the best use of available information unless we know how to create new patterns and escape from the dominance of the old ones. Vertical thinking is concerned with proving or developing concept patterns. Lateral thinking is concerned with restructuring such patterns (insight) and provoking new ones (creativity).[5]

HOLOGRAMS AND GAMES

Another example that explains the meaning of paradigm is the hologram, a picture or word that is not easily seen at first glance. Only after the brain has adjusted to the image is the picture or word "seen." Evidently, our brain uses old information to process new and unfamiliar data.

Paradigms are like that. It is not enough just to see with our physical eyes. Our brain uses old information and patterns to process new experiences. This is why we are often brain dead to an innovation. We cannot process a new idea until there is a paradigm shift in our thinking about the new body of information.

A game is another type of paradigm. It has its own rules, boundaries and objects that determine the course of events. Without these paradigm factors, the players would not know how to play and the activity would turn into chaos. For instance, suppose a United States football team and a European football team were going to play "football." The United States football team would use its rules, and the opposing team would play according to what the rest of the world calls football—soccer. Obviously, not a lot would be accomplished. The game could not even start because two different sets of rules and equipment would be used. A paradigm shift changes the rules, boundaries and objects associated with existing situations.

SWISS WATCHMAKERS MISSED THE SHIFT

According to Joel Barker, an expert in paradigm change, from 1979 to 1982, employment in Swiss watchmaking dropped from sixty-five thousand to fifteen thousand. The invention of the quartz watch caused the sudden collapse of a world industry. How did it happen?

The research division of the Swiss watchmaking industry invented the quartz watch, and in 1967 presented the concept and the first prototype to their board. The owners and administrators weren't interested! Their thinking required gears and springs in watches. This new quartz approach didn't fit their idea (paradigm) of a watch. This is what happened in that meeting:

The main villain proved to be the inflexibility of Swiss watch-makers. They simply refused to adjust to one of the biggest technological changes in the history of time keeping, the development of the electronic watch. Swiss companies were so tied to the traditional technology that they couldn't . . . or wouldn't . . . see the opportunities offered by the electronic revolution.[6]

At an international watch congress two companies, Seiko and Texas Instruments, saw the Swiss demonstrate the quartz electronic watch. These smaller companies, who were new to the watchmaking business, thought laterally and saw potential in the new idea. When they began to manufacture and market the electronic watch, the Swiss were left behind. The paradigm had changed. This illustration helps us understand the importance of a paradigm to both those who have the "eyes" to see and those who do not.

PARADIGM MISCALCULATIONS

MURPHY'S LAW ARCHIVES;
Case No. 48732; Ref: AB-5634297

Ms. S. Brown, Administrator
Allied Insurance Company
347 Worth Street
Akron, Ohio 43256

Dear Ms. Brown,

This is a response to your request for additional information in Block number 3 of the referenced accident reporting form where I put "Poor planning" as the cause of my accident. You said in your letter that I should explain this more fully, and I trust that the following details will be sufficient.

I am a bricklayer by trade. On the day of the accident, I was working alone on the roof of a new six-story building. In the late afternoon, when I had completed my work, I discovered that I had about 500 pounds of bricks left over. Rather than carry them down by hand, I decided to lower them in a barrel using a pulley which, fortunately, was already attached to a beam protruding from the side of the building at roof level. After securing the rope at ground level, I returned to the roof and loaded the 500 pounds of bricks into the barrel. Then I went back down to the ground and untied the rope and held onto it rather tightly to insure a slow decent of the barrel of bricks. You will note in Block number 11 of the accident form that I weigh 135 pounds.

Due to my surprise at being jerked off the ground so suddenly, I lost my presence of mind and forgot to let go of the rope. Perhaps needless to say, I proceeded at a rather rapid rate up the side of the building. In the vicinity of the third floor, I met the barrel coming down. This is when I broke my left arm and collarbone. Slowed only slightly, I continued my rapid accent, not stopping until I cracked my skull on the beam and ran the fingers of my right hand two knuckles into the pulley. I had regained my presence of mind by this time, however, and held tightly onto the rope in spite of my pain.

At approximately the same time, the barrel hit the ground and its bottom fell out depositing the bricks in a ragged pile. Devoid of the weight of the bricks, the barrel weighed something less than fifty pounds. (I refer you again to Box number 11.) As you may have already guessed, I then began a rapid descent down the side of the building. In the vicinity of the third floor, I met the barrel coming up. This accounts for the lacerations on my legs and lower body. The encounter with the barrel slowed me enough to lessen my injuries when I fell onto the pile of bricks and fortunately, only one ankle was broken. The puncture wounds on my chest and stomach came as I lay on the bricks unable to move. Staring up at the barrel, I again lost my presence of mind and let go of the rope. Following the advice of my doctor, I am planning to leave the bricklaying trade and pursue a less dangerous occupation.

Yours truly, _____

As you read this comedy of errors, when did you suspect the bricklayer had made a serious paradigm mistake? His first paradigm mistake told him he, whose weight was 135 pounds, could lower the 500 pound barrel of bricks with a rope. The second mistake was holding onto the rope, which also seems a logical survival reaction when suspended in space. The chain reaction of events resulted from those innocent looking decisions. This story speaks of a broad principle in life we all have lived out in one way or another: most of us have held onto our own "barrels of bricks" that outweighed us, and we have suffered the consequences.

Someone suggested the events described in the previous letter do not illustrate a paradigm shift as much as stupidity. Of course in hindsight, holding on to any wrong idea looks stupid. However, at the time, holding on to the rope often looks perfectly logical, possibly even astute. Ask the Swiss watchmakers!

LET GO OF THE ROPE, BEFORE IT'S TOO LATE!

A New Testament picture of the church is being recreated before our very eyes. God's incarnational paradigm (God's presence, power and purpose lived out with His people) is once again being applied to the world as we know it.

Not every church will enter into this new paradigm. When the dust settles in the next decade, some churches and denominations will be the Swiss watchmaking industry of the church world. God will use other churches and groups as dramatic instruments of a new/old spiritual revolution. Those with "old-brain thinking" will not enter into the spiritual revolution exploding all around them.

History teaches us God is not held hostage by any group, denomination, institution or established leadership. As Jesus told the religionist Nicodemus, "The wind blows where it wills . . ." No man can control it. God uses whoever He desires, whenever He chooses. If the established and recognized institutions will not respond to God's new way of doing things, He will always find others who will. More likely than not, new paradigms will offend and seem unorthodox to those like Nicodemus who heard Jesus' words and said, "How can these things be?" In fact, God's remnant always looks a little ragtag and wild. As you look at your present paradigm for the church, you must be willing to ask yourself, "What am I holding on to that God is in the process of changing?"

2

THE TWO-WINGED CHURCH

Perhaps the church, in many areas, must be smaller
before it can be substantially stronger.
—Elton Trueblood

I n 1989, God brought me back from fifteen years of church planting in Thailand to the United States to "begin a different kind of church." After a year of trial and error, I found myself in Houston working with Dr. Ralph Neighbour. Because of my association with him, other desperate souls began contacting me about this new kind of church. For some reason they thought I knew more than they, which was debatable.

A group of young men from Texas A & M University came to talk with me about the church. After telling them all I knew, I still felt inadequate in explaining this twentieth century phenomenon in its true simplicity. Before they left, we joined hands and prayed together. These young men, still in their 20's, had a vision of the church which had only come to me at the age of 50. As they left, God gave me a story. I share it in every conference I teach because it paints a macro picture of what many call the "cell church."

THE TWO-WINGED CHURCH

The Creator once created a church with two wings: one wing was for large group celebration, the other wing was for small group community.

Using both wings, the church could soar high into the heavens, entering into His presence and do His will over all the earth.

After a few hundred years of flying across the earth, the Two-Winged Church began to question the need for the small group wing. The jealous, wicked serpent who had no wings, loudly applauded this idea. Over the years, the small group wing became weaker and weaker from lack of exercise until it virtually had no strength at all. The Two-Winged church that had soared high in the heavens was now for all practical purposes one-winged.

The Creator of the church was very sad. He knew the Two-Winged design had allowed the church to soar into His presence and do His bidding. Now with only one wing, just lifting off of the ground required tremendous energy and effort. And if the church did manage to become airborne, it was prone to fly in circles, lose its sense of direction, and not fly very far from its take off point. Spending more and more time in the safety and comfort of its habitat, it grew contented with an earth bound existence.

From time to time, the church dreamed of flying into the presence of the Creator, and doing His work over all the earth. But now, the strong large group wing controlled every movement of the church and doomed it to an earth-bound existence.

In compassion, the Creator finally stretched forth his hand and reshaped His church so it could use both wings. Once again the Creator possessed a church that could fly into His presence and soar high over all the earth, fulfilling His purposes and plans.

WELCOME TO THE CELL CHURCH

I hear two consistent thoughts about the church from Christians all over the world: "The church as we know it is not the church we see in the New Testament" and, "small groups have something to do with getting the church running right." Many see the traditional ways as an old wineskin, no longer able to contain the new wine of the gospel. Even those most comfortable with traditionally accepted church patterns often wish it could be:

- less isolated from the world in which it lives
- more relevant to the needs of society
- more compassionate in the way it uses money and manpower
- reaching more people instead of promoting better programs

• less materialistic with its huge buildings and debts
• more redemptive and less political
• and less influenced by the world it is called to influence

Is there an alternative to the traditional design of the church? A growing number of Christians are convinced God is recreating the wineskin of the New Testament church. This church lives together in community and is today called the "cell church."

What does the cell church look like? Dr. Ralph Neighbour included the following working definition of a cell church in the *Cell Church Magazine:*

> The human body is made up of millions of cells, the basic unit of life. Likewise, Cells form the basic unit of the Cell Church. Believers actively seek relationships with God, each other and unbelievers in Cell Groups of 5-15 people. These relationships stimulate each member to maturity in worship, mutual edification and evangelism. This is Community . . . .
>
> Built on the principle that all Christians are ministers and that the work of ministry should be performed by every Christian, the Cell Church actively seeks to develop each disciple into the likeness of Christ. The Cell Groups are the very forum for ministry, equipping, and evangelism.
>
> Cells also cluster together for weekly or biweekly "Congregation" meetings and "Celebrations." While these meetings are important, the focus of the church is fixed on the weekly Cell meetings in homes. The reason? This is where love, community, relationships, ministry, and evangelism spring up naturally and powerfully. Therefore, the life of the church is in the Cells, not in a building. The church is a dynamic, organic, spiritual being that can only be lived out in the lives of believers in community.[1]

SEVEN TESTS TO HELP IDENTIFY A NEW TESTAMENT CHURCH

Many churches have small groups of from five to fifteen or more people meeting weekly as one of their programs. Does this classify them as a cell church? The following tests help differentiate between cell churches and those which may have similar structures and terminology but possess a different dynamic.

1. The institutional test: Is the church a living *organism* or an *organization?* If you were to do away with the building and the Sunday morning meeting, could the church survive? If the church would survive without a building and Sunday morning meetings, it passes the first test for a New Testament cell church.

2. The cell test: Is a small group (referred to in this book as a cell) considered the church in nature, purpose and power? Does the church see the small group as the basic Christian community and the essential unit of the church? If leaders and people would cringe at referring to the small group as the church, then that church is not a New Testament cell church. Paul himself had no problem calling groups in the homes churches.

3. The photocopy test: When the model is reproduced, is the new church as clear and bright as the original? Will the model transfer? If the church replicates itself with only dimmer versions of itself, then it is not a New Testament cell church. This is not a *numerical* test, but a test of *nature* and *life*. Does it consistently reproduce the dynamic of the original?

4. The simplicity test: Is the church fragmented and complex? As it grows larger, does it get more complex or less complex? Does it take a CEO to make it work? A cell church will continue to operate through its simple cell leadership structure even if the governing administrative framework disappears. Even with the presence of large numbers of members and leaders, the cell church will have a simplicity about how it operates.

5. The multiplication test: Does the church show hope of multiplying? Is a structure in place through which dynamic growth could happen? Or is the strategy based on addition of new members? A cell church can systematically multiply because the point of growth takes place at the integrated cell level, not through compartmentalized multiple programs.

6. The adult test: Does the church reach new adult converts, or is the church sustained by transfer growth from other churches and biological growth by baptizing its own children? An operating cell church will reach new adult converts.

7. The persecution test: Will the church survive if it is forced underground? Could the kind of small groups attached to our church programs survive persecution without the institutional cushion? The cell church will survive through its New Testament cells no matter what happens politically, socially, economically or internally.

ETHIOPIA

One church that passed these tests was started by the Mennonite Church of America in Ethiopia. By the 1970's, the Western missionaries had returned home, leaving an indigenous national church of 5000 members. In 1982, the Communists overthrew the government of Ethiopia. Persecution of the church began. The Mennonite churches had all of their buildings and property confiscated. Many of their leaders were imprisoned, and the members were forbidden to meet. The church went underground without leaders, without buildings, without the opportunity to meet together publically or to use any of their public programs. While underground, they could not even sing out loud for fear of someone reporting them to the authorities.

Ten years later in 1992, the Communist government was overthrown, allowing this church to come out of hiding. Church leaders decided to gather all remaining members together for services. Needless to say, they were surprised to find that the 5,000 members had grown to over 50,000 in the ten year period!

This story illustrates the power of the cell. Christ designed the church to survive in its most basic life form. This was true in the first century church, and it is true of the church today. Everywhere the church has been forced underground into a small group structure it has survived, and more often than not it has grown. Will the church enter into its New Testament small group structure only in communist countries and times of persecution? It might appear so. However, at this particular time in history, God is restoring the cell unit as the principle structure of the church even in countries free from persecution.

A PEEK AT THE TWO-WINGED CHURCH

I have gathered more than twenty key characteristics to explain the structure and dynamic of the cell church. This list is not exhaustive, but along with the other definitions in this chapter, it will give you a more complete picture of the nature of cell churches. While generally true, every characteristic will not be found in every cell church. Likewise, some traditional churches may exhibit a combination of these characteristics.

- The cell church Jesus designed operates as the church not only on Sunday, but on the other six days of the week as well.

- The cell church may have a building, but the building is functional and not sacred.
- The growth of the church doesn't depend on how much square footage can be financed and provided. The building formula of the cell church is: grow and then build.
- Cells or small groups of Christians meet in homes during the week and are the basic unit of the church.
- These cells act as the "delivery system" of the church through which cell members live out the gospel in the world.
- Every member of the church receives equipping for the work of the ministry in these small groups.
- Celebration worship on Sunday overflows from the body life taking place during the week in the lives of members.
- Members are accountable to each other.
- The cell church produces large numbers of servant leaders who enable the work of ministry to take place at the basic cell level.
- In the small groups, members take off their masks and receive edification and healing. Real New Testament fellowship takes place.
- The "one another" passages found in the New Testament have a context in which they can be experienced.
- The church centered in home cells is designed to survive persecution.
- The lost are reached through cell friendship evangelism.
- Spiritual gifts essential for edification, equipping and evangelism are released in the natural setting of the cells.
- Full-time leaders are set aside for prayer and to seek God's face for the body.
- Multiplication of cells, converts, disciples and leaders constantly occurs.
- Operating cell churches have a dramatic impact upon the society. Their small groups touch the hurts and needs in the world around them.
- Leaders and pastors provide oversight, vision, and accountability for leaders of the cell groups.
- More money is available for ministry and missions as each member matures in their understanding of stewardship as a lifestyle.
- The community of cells is a place of healing for the individual and the family.
- The administration of the church is simplified around the basic cell

unit. This significantly reduces the multiple programs necessary to run a traditional church.

• Primary care for members is provided at the cell level instead of the professional staff level.

• Ephesians 4:12 works! Leaders "equip the saints for the work of ministry."

Defined at the Cell Level

The key to understanding the cell church is the cell itself and what Robert Banks calls the "church-like" character of base communities. (Chapter 13 explores the nature of the cell in greater detail.) The Brazilian theologian, J.B. Libanio, gives the following description of the cell or base community.

> They are not a movement, an association or a religious congregation . . . They are not a method (or the only method) of building up the church: they are the church itself. They are not a miraculous recipe for all the ills of society and the church. They are the church renewing itself . . . They are not a utopia; they are a sign of the kingdom, though they are not the kingdom . . . They are not messianic, but they can be prophetic and produce prophets like the church should. They are not a natural . . . community . . . identified with a race, language, people, family . . . They are the church . . . They are not a protest group, although their life is a protest against the mediocrity, sloth and inauthenticity of many . . . They are not special groups for special people. They are the church committed to the ordinary man, to the poor, to those who suffer injustice . . . They are not closed: they are open to dialogue with all. They are not a reform of anything in pastoral work: they are a decisive pastoral option, made in order to construct a new image of the church.[2]

If you want to understand and identify a cell church, look at the cells. The small group defines a cell church. Everything that happens in a cell church—the weekly celebrations, harvest events, training and equipping retreats, camps, meetings for oversight—exists to support the cells. Everything relates out from and back to the basic cell community.

EAT THE BANANA

How can the taste of a banana be described to a person who had never seen one? To truly understand how a banana tastes, at some point the descriptions must become experiential. It is best to peel the banana, give it to the person and say, "Here, taste it for yourself."

Even with these definitions and illustrations, you may still wonder what the cell church looks like. This is normal because, like the taste of a banana, the church is something we can only know *experientially.* No matter how much we understand the church theologically and academically, the one who best understands the definition of a "cell church" is the one most involved in experiencing it. The cell church is not something to simply study and analyze. At some point, our definition of church must be experienced and lived out.

3
LARRY: A LEADERSHIP PARADIGM

One of the tragedies of our time is that
the minister is both overworked and unemployed.
—Samuel Miller

L arry, a church leader in his forties, had already pastored several successful churches but had grown increasingly disillusioned with the traditional, one-day-a-week church. He listened as others attending the conference shared the stock answer about why they had come: "I have come to learn more about the cell church." When his time came, Larry got "gut honest." He shared his hunger to find answers about how the church could be New Testament. With a great deal of feeling and obvious pain, he revealed, "If I don't find some answers, I'm going fishing."

Everyone in the room knew instantly what he meant and roared with laughter. Larry was going to find something else to do if the situation didn't change. More of us than just Larry had already considered the same course of action.

For every vocal "Larry," scores of silent "Larrys" are trying to survive in the traditional church with as much dignity and honesty as possible. Larry is one of the thousands of pastors living in the pain of leading churches that do not measure up to the church paradigm God has placed in their hearts. Their picture of the church will never be satisfied with a one-day-a-week design.

OVERWORKED AND UNEMPLOYED

Pastoring a traditional, one-winged church is one of the most difficult jobs on earth. Of course, it has many rewards as well. In the three pastorates I held before going overseas, I experienced much joy and happiness. In many ways it's a great job—helping people, talking about Jesus, ministering to people in the important times of their lives, giving spiritual and moral direction to the community.

However, over the past several years, I have seen in leaders such as Larry a picture of the church which doesn't measure up, despite all the good works and the pastor's efforts. How can there be such burnout and frustration attached to this special calling? I'm convinced the dream and expectation kill us. The vision of the church in our hearts doesn't match the reality of the church in the world. The church we preach *to* on Sunday is not like the church we preach *about* on Sunday. Deep down we know something is wrong.

This is why the pastor of a Sunday-dominated church, in the words of Samuel Miller, is at once "overworked and unemployed:"

> Overworked in a multitude of tasks that do not have the slightest connection with religion, and unemployed in the exacting labors and serious concerns of maintaining a disciplined spiritual life among mature men and women. . . . Whatever the current ideal of the minister comes from—the big operator, the smart salesman, the successful tycoon—it still remains a puzzle why the minister should fall prey to such false images unless he has completely confused what he is supposed to be doing.[1]

Why do we have this confusion among leaders who are gifted and called to pastor? They are educated specifically for that purpose, and are sincere in their desire to serve God.

The church's most creative and visionary leaders pay a terrible price because they long to soar, but preside over an earthbound church. God has placed the same church vision that He gave to Paul in Ephesians, in the hearts of leaders of every age. According to Paul, the church is the "fullness of God," the "power of God," the "wisdom of God," the "household of God," the "temple of God," the "body of God," and the "glory of God."

Those are not words most people associate with the church of the twentieth century. Maybe we would dare to use those words about the "raptured" church in heaven, but not the "ruptured" church we are part of on earth. The church we know, despite all the good things, just doesn't work like the New Testament model and therein lies the agony of pastor and members alike.

BETTER TO SHATTER A DREAM THAN CONCEAL THE TRUTH

A museum began to clean a seventeenth century painting supposedly by an old master. During the cleaning process a fleck of paint came off, then another and another. The experts watched in horror as a layer of outside paint began disintegrating before their eyes. But underneath they discovered another painting. A later artist had tried to improve the original masterpiece. Now they saw the truth. This was the original, and it was much more valuable and important. The outer layer that had been added was carefully removed until the original picture was restored and displayed in a prominent place in the museum. "It is better to shatter a dream than conceal the truth!"[2]

Small flecks of the painting of the only church I knew started coming off very early in my ministry. From time to time, some new book or program promised hope of a different kind of church. I would eagerly try to implement the new idea, but the results never came close to duplicating either the spirit or results of the New Testament church.

Over the years, my wife Mary and I enjoyed brainstorming at conventions and on other special occasions with Max and Katie Brown, special friends from college and seminary. Our discussions often turned to new and innovative concepts about the church. Max first told me about Ralph Neighbour's experimental church in Houston in the late 1960s. The idea of reaching the hurting and lost in the world through caring ministry groups seemed so New Testament, so right, and so different from what was happening in our own churches.

Unfortunately, when we returned home after our convention conversations, we entered the one-winged church realm that demanded all our energy just to keep the good activities and programs in motion. Our hearts might have belonged to the New Testament church, but our bodies were owned by the one-winged, traditional church paradigm.

In 1972, during a Lay Renewal Weekend, I experienced New Testament fellowship and small group body life for the first time. Visiting teams of excited "lay people" stayed in the homes of our members. The weekend was built around small group encounters and a lot of honest sharing. New songs were sung *to* God, not *about* Him. Lives were transformed and marriages were healed. Christ in our midst, working in power, remains the underlying impression of that weekend. That experience applied some pretty strong paint remover to my old picture of the church.

I had already been vitally connected to the church for thirty years before getting my first taste of real New Testament body life. Although I had experienced many high spiritual moments in the church, nothing so genuinely New Testament in flavor compared to those brief moments of small group life.

Unfortunately, I didn't have a clue about what to do with the fruit of that experience. So I poured it right back into the only wineskin I had: my traditional church wineskin. Although, that weekend of New Testament community had significant impact upon several individual lives, including mine, it didn't make much of an impact upon my traditional church. It was eventually chewed up and spit out in a form our traditional programs could tolerate.

THE ONE-WINGED CHURCH IN BANGKOK

Other parts of the painting began to fall from the canvas from the moment I arrived as a new missionary at the Bangkok airport on January 1, 1975. Mary, twins Joey and Jimmy, Matt, Juleigh and I stepped off of the plane into unbelievable heat and humidity, pollution thick enough to see, and traffic patterns deserving the word *kamikaze*. This was a whole new world. We had entered the "twilight zone" of culture shock, Bangkok style!

The culture shock did not last long. Our children adapted quickly, and to them Thailand became home with special people, places and experiences. Mary and I learned to communicate in the language, to read the Thai Bible and the road signs, to relate culturally to the Thai people, and to eat some of the hottest but most delicious food in the world.

I survived culture shock, but never really got over my "church/mission shock." God called me into urban church planting and gave me a passion to discover a strategy for reproducing New Testament Churches in urban settings. This zeal soon conflicted with reality as I became acquainted with the church in Thailand.

The church building architecture was different, the signs on church walls were written in a strange language, the songs were sung in a minor key, and the literature was produced in a different format. However, I quickly realized this church was little different in kind and nature from the one I had left back home. This was just the First Church of Everytown, USA transplanted into Bangkok, Thailand. Even if one did not understand the language, it was possible to guess the order of Sunday service, and unfortunately, church business meetings operated just the same!

Somehow, I had expected the church in one of the least Christian cities in the world to be different in nature, more New Testament in function, more dynamic in power and more focused in thrust. I began to suspect something was seriously flawed in my church model. From my current perspective, I know this was just another one-winged-church, Thai style! It took me more than fifteen years to realize my familiar and comfortable church paradigm could not reproduce in Thailand the vision of the church God had placed in my heart.

I was driven back to the New Testament to find a more biblical picture of the church than the one I was using. Elton Trueblood puts this search in proper perspective:

True recovery is never a matter of going backward for the sake of re-establishing an older pattern, but rather of uncovering what has been hidden or overlaid and therefore forgotten. The purpose of such uncovering is the potential effect upon the present and the future. We go back to the New Testament, therefore, not as antiquarians and not as mere historians, but in the hope of finding hints of vitality of which our time is relatively unaware.[3]

WE DON'T WANT FAKES

Alfred I. DuPont, former head of the DuPont corporation, was approached by a Philadelphia dealer claiming to have a portrait of DuPont's great-great-grandmother holding her infant son. The asking price was $25,000. When DuPont refused, noting the presence of two artistic styles in the portrait, the dealer dropped the price to $10,000, then $1,000, and, in desperation, $400, which duPont accepted, believing the frame to be worth that much. A curator at the Philadelphia Museum examined the painting and found that 18th-century clothing had been painted over the subjects' original 17th-century apparel. After removing the new paint, the curator discovered that the original work was by Murillo; the $400 painting was reassessed at $150,000.[4]

Some fakes are very good. When caught, forgers ask, "Why make such a big deal about the original? If the fake fooled you, then it is just as good as the original painting." The writer of the above article explains the difference between a fake and the genuine article: "Art experts counter with the claim that, over time, a fake reveals a 'deadness' while a master's original keeps unveiling facets of inspiration—the painter's genius keeps the artwork alive."[5]

That is why it is better to "shatter a dream rather than conceal the truth" about everything—especially the church. The original vibrates with life while the imitation is a dead thing. Jesus was the Master Painter. His picture of the church keeps unveiling facets of inspiration.

HOW DO CHURCH LEADERS SURVIVE?

Some church leaders survive by pretending they are really flying like the New Testament church. Living in their own spiritual fantasy world, where everything is always wonderful, they choose to live a lie rather than to shatter their dream. These are some of the most vocal defenders of the traditional church and bitter opponents of the cell church. They cannot allow their dream to be shattered.

Other pastors, in alarming numbers, become so disillusioned they leave the ministry for counseling, teaching or denominational offices that at least give some reasonable hope of producing the results for which they were designed. These vocations are just as important as pastoring (if one is called to them) however, they are poor substitutes for a frustrated leader who has really been called to pastor.

Still others learn to live with the damaged picture that is left and make the best of it. But it takes its toll in feelings of frustration, anger, hurt, and hopelessness. Leaders feel used and families suffer.

Gerald Kennedy tells the story of an Arabic man who felt hungry one night, lit a candle, and opened a date. It was wormy, and he threw it aside. He tried another, and it also had worms. So did a third. Whereupon, he blew out the candle and ate the fourth one. Rather than face unpleasant realities, we often find it easier to remain in darkness. Not only can physical arteries harden, but a man's spiritual outlook may become stiff and unbending as well.[6]

Those of us in the church can choose to turn out the light and remain in darkness concerning what God is doing today. In that way, we don't have to face unpleasant realities. Standing in the darkness, I have eaten my share of wormy dates over the past several decades! Today, I am no longer satisfied with either the darkness, or strange tasting fruit.

IS MY FINGER IN IT?

In his book *Disciple*, Juan Carlos Ortiz tells about his church experience in Buenos Aires. He began with 184 members and after two years had grown to 600. In his words, his "Sunday School was tops," and his follow-up system "was one of the best." His denomination was so impressed, they invited him to speak at two different conventions. He commented:

> Yet underneath it all, I sensed that something wasn't right. Things seemed to stay high so long as I worked sixteen hours a day. But when I relaxed, everything came down. . . . I headed for the countryside and gave myself to meditation and prayer.
>
> The Holy Spirit began to break me down. The first thing He said was, "Juan, that thing you have is not a church. It's a business." I didn't understand what He meant. "You are promoting the gospel the same way Coca-Cola sells Coke," He said, "the same way *Reader's Digest* sells books and magazines. You are using all the human tricks you learned in school. But where is My finger in all of this?"
>
> I didn't know what to say. I had to admit that my congregation was more of a business enterprise than a spiritual body.
>
> Then the Lord told me a second thing. "You are not growing," He said. "You think you are, because you've gone from 200 to 600. But you're not growing—you're just getting fat." What did that mean? "All you have is more people of the same quality as before. No one is maturing; the level remains the same. Before, you had 200 spiritual babies; now you have 600 spiritual babies."[7]

The pertinent question about our church is not how large it is, but "Where is God's finger in all of this?" Ultimately, this is the only question that can define a Christian leader's sense of fulfillment and satisfaction about His ministry.

Dangerous Memories

Johann Baptist Metz challenges us to consider memories from the past:

> There are dangerous memories, memories which make demands on us. There are memories in which earlier experiences break through to the centre-point of our lives and reveal new and dangerous insights for the present. . . . Such memories are like dangerous and incalculable visitations from the past. They are memories that we have to take into account, memories, as it were, with a future content.[8]

God is planting the seed of a different kind of church in our hearts. For many, the new feelings about the church come first, and then the search to understand and explain those feelings follows. God speaks His vision into the hearts of His people, and then confirms the vision through special innovators who verbalize or model the vision. These "feelings" are "dangerous memories" from the past that have a "future content."

As we enter the twenty-first century God is re-creating His Two-Winged Church. What happens on Sunday in gathered meetings is not enough for those with a vision for living together in small group fellowship and body life during the week.

The men and women of Acts also began with vision, memories and dreams. The first sermon in the first century revolutionary church began with a quote about such things:

> And it shall be in the last days, God says,
> That I will pour forth of My Spirit upon all mankind;
> And your sons, and your daughters shall prophesy,
> And your young men shall see visions,
> And your old men shall dream dreams (Acts 2:17).

These were dangerous memories from the mouth of the prophet Joel, and from the heart of God. God had kept these memories alive through more than five centuries until finally, in the fullness of time, He stirred them into the hearts of His people. Dangerous memories produce dangerous men and women, who act out their dreams and make them possible. Such were the men and women of the early church. Do not be surprised with the memories and feelings stirring within you. Listen to them and let God stir them to life. They are the seeds of *The Second Reformation*.

4

EDDIE: THE PARADIGM
FROM THE PEW

The basic trouble [with the church] is that the proposed
cure has such a striking similarity to the disease.
—Elton Trueblood

enry G. Bosch tells the amusing story of what happened when a
customer in a small store discovered that "Eddie," the slow-
moving clerk, was not around.

"Where's Eddie? Is he sick?"

"Nope," came the reply. "He ain't workin' here no more."

"Do you have anyone in mind for the vacancy?" inquired the
customer.

"Nope! Eddie didn't leave no vacancy!"

There are quite a few "Eddies" in most churches today. They
leave, and no one even notices. Why? First, because there is no
real sense of the Body of Christ in which members are involved
in a functioning manner. Second, many, by their own decision,
have chosen to sit on the church bench on the sidelines of the
action.[1]

Bosch is describing a prevailing characteristic of the modern institutional church. A large percentage of church members (often estimated to
be 80% or more) contribute little to the life and ministry of the church.

The "Eddie-fication" of the Church

After introducing Eddie at a conference in Canada, a written question appeared on the front table during one of the breaks. It read: "Could it be that Constantine was the cause of the *Eddie-fication* of the church?" We got a big laugh out of that, but it was a keen insight as well as a clever pun. We are indeed victims of Constantine's Eddie-fication of the church.

By 312 A.D., the church had changed from regular home meetings and large group meetings to almost exclusively conducting meetings in special buildings. Consequently, the church became an audience! Since that time many things have differed from church to church, theological interpretation, type of worship and even clothes clergy wear. But the one-winged, cathedral *structure* has remained constant over the past seventeen centuries of church history.

While Constantine gave the ultimate stamp of approval to this one-winged approach, it was not completely his fault. Several trends developed during the first 300 years of church history, making the fourth century ripe for Satan's attack and Constantine's mistake. God's people were gradually being trapped in an institutional rather than an incarnational wineskin because of the following factors:

- Christianity was more and more aligned with political systems.
- Professional leaders were developing church structure.
- Spiritual power had given way to human ability and effort.
- Servant leadership was gradually replaced with authoritarianism.
- Church structure was being patterned after the world.
- The church was on the defensive rather than the offensive.
- The small group context of the church was suspect in the eyes of government.

We may not know all that was happening during the years 100-300 A.D., but we do see the finished product in Constantine's cathedral church.

The One-Winged Cathedral Design

Using a combination of the Roman governmental and feudal systems, Emperor Constantine developed a church structure that has lasted for seventeen centuries. What are the characteristics of Constantine's cathedral paradigm?

- People go to a building (cathedral)
- on a special day of the week (Sunday)
- and someone (a priest, or today, a pastor)
- does something to them (teaching, preaching, absolution or healing)
- or for them (a ritual or entertainment)
- for a price (offerings)

By building cathedrals and placing rituals and leadership within those buildings, Constantine changed the very nature and life of the church as originally designed by Christ. The changes grew out of new ways of thinking about God's church as an *organization* rather than as an *organism*. The change in structure reflects a fundamental change in how the church related to God and how God could relate to the church. The changes were first of all theological—then structural.

In a recent seminar someone asked: "How could Constantine's change to the cathedral in the fourth century have had such a profound affect upon the church, even until today?" It was not the *cathedral* that affected the church; it was what the *cathedral approach* did to the *small group context* of the church.

NEUTRALIZING THE CHURCH

Early on, Satan realized he could not destroy the church. Jesus had guaranteed the gates of hell would not prevail against His church. His promise was fulfilled. Persecution, economic hardships, political change, false teachings, pagan religions—none of these were able to slow down the spread of the church in those first centuries. By the third century, an estimated 6,000,000 Christians lived in the Roman Empire alone. Just as Satan could not destroy the incarnate Christ in physical body, he could not destroy the spiritual body of Christ on earth, the church. If Satan couldn't destroy the church, what could he do? He would neutralize it!

Satan could not have devised a more ingenious plan! First of all, he gave the church political sanction and social respectability. Then he set about to neutralize the church by attacking its small group structure. The church was thus limited in its ability to nurture new members, apply spiritual power, edify the body, train necessary leaders, deliver the gospel to the world, encounter the presence of the living Christ and walk in the gifts of the Spirit.

This resulted in a one-winged bird. It still looked like a bird and sounded like a bird, but it would be unable to do the very thing that set it apart as a bird. It could no longer fly! The church became a one-winged, earth-bound religious institution. The balance and strength of His original design was neutralized enough to distort God's primary purposes for the church—edification and evangelism. The church became an audience of Eddies.

FROM PRODUCER TO CONSUMER

A large percentage of church members are consumers, not producers. They are consumer Christians because the traditional church has no viable context in which to make them producers, or use them in a productive way.

Eddie's contract with the traditional church is to be pampered, to receive ministry and to be entertained. In exchange, he will be counted in the numbers and will give an offering from time to time to support the system. Consumer Christians represent 80 percent of church members who are supported and ministered to by the other 20 percent who produce.

This means Eddie is anything but a neutral factor in the ministry of the church. In fact, he probably represents its most serious debilitating factor. Eddie is a major consumer in the church itself, requiring many producing Christians to care for his needs. Consumer Christians neutralize the productivity of the 20 percent of mature members who expend most of their time and energy ministering to Eddie, Mrs. Eddie and all their Little Eddies.

Think about the 20 percent of mature, producing church members. They are capable of reaching out into the world, of modeling New Testament Christian living, of taking the church beyond the church parking lot, of making a difference in the Kingdom. But they are so busy maintaining the system that supports Eddie that little time or energy is left to minister in a New Testament sense.

When all the Eddies sit down on church pews, you can almost hear the sucking sound as they draw ministry to themselves. How many producing Christians would you estimate are required to maintain the kind of program that will attract Eddie and keep him happy in the traditional church? Whatever the number, it is high maintenance and low return on the time, effort and money, because Eddie seldom contributes in a positive way to either the edification of the church or the evangelism of the world.

Eddie may leave if he finds another church he feels meets more of his needs. Eddie will gravitate toward the strongest ministry pull and the most guaranteed benefits. Eddie can always find spiritual sounding reasons to justify his migration to greener pastures. "We are concerned for the spiritual welfare of our family. This new church has such a wonderful program for our children." Or, "Their style of worship is so exciting and moving. We want to worship God like that." Or, "I am fed by the wonderful preaching of that pastor. He is such a spiritual man of God." Who can question Eddie's motives when he gives such spiritual-sounding reasons?

When Eddie leaves, he and his type "leave no vacancy" in the real ministry or work of the church. They just leave an empty spot on a pew on Sunday morning, a little less change in the offering plate and one less member to have to pamper and please. Church leaders then must go out looking for another Eddie or two to replace the ones lost. What is going on here?

CHURCH CONSUMERISM

Churches of all sizes are held hostage by consumer Eddies who are the prime target audience for most twentieth century churches. Indeed, some of the most popular church growth strategies of the past several decades are built around consumer Christians in one way or another. Clever marketing schemes try to attract and hold the Eddies floating around in a self-centered society.

Why has the church agreed to allow its most immature members to dictate the ministry focus of the church? Why does the church tolerate manipulation—practically blackmail—from those members who contribute the least to the work of the church?

Eddie has his hook into the one-winged church because his presence is the measure of success in one-winged church circles. Filling up the church on Sunday morning is the bottom line of institutional religion. The modern institutional church has a "body count" criteria for tracking its success. No matter how many spiritual-sounding phrases we use, success in the traditional church is tied to the number of warm bodies present in a two hour span of time on Sunday morning. And Eddie will not come if we do not minister to him and give him what he wants.

The traditional system, needs Eddie to fill a pew, to be counted in the numbers on Sunday, to financially support the construction of new buildings and the addition of new staff "ministers." All of these hooks are necessary to attract more consumer Eddies, who can fill more pews, which creates a need for new and better buildings to attract more Eddies, which means bigger buildings and on and on the cycle goes. Eddie is the driving force behind the "noses and nickels" game of the traditional church.

Eutychus, a fictional contributor to *Christianity Today*, describes his church's experience with church consumerism:

Fear of Flying?

Our church, jumping into the new world of evangelism via niche marketing, has recently begun reaching out to an underserved target group: the frequent flyer. Because so many people in our upscale community travel throughout the week, we spared no expense.

Our seats have individual air-conditioner nozzles, reading lights, and usher call buttons. A seat-belt sign comes on automatically when the preacher starts to say something controversial; oxygen masks and airsickness bags are located in the pew racks.

Our "Frequent Attender Plan" rewards consistent attendance with discounts toward overseas travel (to the Holy Land, of course). Our "First Class" seating pampers those who make generous contributions to the church building fund by allowing them to exit the service during the last verse of the closing hymn.

After a few months, however, things have started to get out of hand. Some of our "frequent flyer" newcomers have begun making requests for special treatment: They want vegetarian meals and alternatives to sermons provided on headsets, and pillows and blankets.

How far should we be willing to go? The elders met last Wednesday and decided to create an ad-hoc committee to consider the newcomers' special requests. Niche-market evangelism is great. But where do you draw the line?[2]

THE DANGER OF DISTRIBUTION SYSTEMS

When the church ceased to meet in small groups and went exclusively to a large group setting, the meaning of "membership" was turned upside down. The church became a channel for the distribution of resources to members rather than challenging members to become resources. Lyle Schaller points out the danger of a distribution, rather than a contribution, world view in an organization.

> The higher the expectations of what people can and will contribute in terms of talent, creativity, time, energy, sacrifices, money, commitment, and other resources, the higher the morale of the total group and the less pronounced the internal divisiveness. That is the message of the Christian faith, the story of the great schools, the theme of the great churches, and the glue of unified societies.
>
> By contrast, raising the expectations of what people will be given invariably tends to politicize the decision-making processes, increase the stress level, and encourage divisive arguments about who is receiving a fair share and who is being cheated out of a fair share.[3]

President John F. Kennedy's famous quote from his inaugural address caught the imagination of the nation in the 1960's because it spoke directly to these two world views. "Ask not what your country can do for you [distribution world view], but what you can do for your country [contribution world view]."

Elton Trueblood saw the necessity for Christians to be an "instrument for the redemption of the world" rather than recipients of benefits:

> When the doctrine of expendability is fully accepted, it becomes at once obvious that, in contrast to many organizations, the Church is not instituted for the benefit of its members. Christ enlists ordinary men and women into His enduring fellowship, not primarily in order to save them, but because He has work for them to do. It is a genuine revelation that His primary call to commitment, "Come to me," is associated at once with a call to labor, "Take my yoke upon you." The Church is essential to the Christian, not because it brings him personal advancement or even inspiration, but because, with all its failures, it is an indispensable instrument for the redemption of the world.[4]

FROM CONSUMER TO PRODUCER

The one-winged church is mass producing Eddie consumers rather than producers. How can we get our members involved? How can we close the back door to the church? What should we do about our most faithful members who are burning out? These are all Eddie questions.

Christian bookstores have shelves packed with discipleship books designed to transform Eddie from a consumer to a producer. Over the past thirty years, the church has tried every discipling scheme known to man to train Eddie to produce. Leaders and producing Christians have spent countless hours trying to change Eddie without success.

Once in a while, an Eddie will make the leap from consumer to producer, but this occurs so rarely that one suspects that particular Eddie was really a closet producer in the first place. Eddie can sit in Sunday School and be a spectator at worship for thirty years and still not be able to pray in public. Ministering or witnessing to someone is out of the question. Using traditional methods, few Eddies can be blasted out of church consumerism into productive Christian ministry.

Many leaders are convinced this Eddie cycle can't be broken without some kind of change in the way the church operates. What is the paradigm shift that will change this frustrating consumer mentality? In order for the church to return to dynamic New Testament Christianity, two things must happen:

1. Get Eddie off the backs of the 20% of church members who are producing Christians so they can penetrate the lost world with the gospel.
2. Change "consumer Christians" into "producing Christians" so they are part of the solution rather than part of the problem.

Jesus designed the church with a small group context in order to make the Eddies of the church a productive part of the body of Christ. No wonder we see so few Eddies in the pages of the New Testament. Eddie couldn't hide behind activities taking place in huge buildings. The first century church met in small home groups, maybe even in Eddie's home. Eddie *had* to participate and produce.

Who is at fault? Eddie? Church leaders? Producing Christians? No! *It is the system!* The system produces consumer Eddies instead of developing Eddie into a producer. Eddie is a victim of a system he did not develop and that cannot prepare him to be anything other than a spiritual parasite.

As early as the 1950's, Elton Trueblood understood something was seriously wrong with church leadership and membership. Trueblood felt a "radical change of some kind" was required. That radical change had to come at the point of the "ordinary" Christian. He quotes John R. Mott:

> A multitude of laymen are today in serious danger. It is positively perilous for them to hear more sermons, attend more Bible classes and open forums and read more religious and ethical works, unless accompanying it all there be afforded day by day an adequate outlet for their new-found truth.[5]

That "outlet" for living out "new-found truth" is the home cell group! Without it, Eddie will never be successfully integrated into the ministry of the church and will continue to be a major obstacle for the edification of the church and the evangelization of the world.

OTHER CHANGES

In addition to changing the nature of membership, virtually every part of the church was affected by the church paradigm shift in the fourth century. Listed below are changes which occurred when the church stopped meeting in small groups and became an audience in large groups:

- *The Lord's Supper changed* from a common meal to a ceremony.
- *Worship changed* from participation to observation.
- *Witness changed* from relationship to salesmanship.
- *Ministry changed* from personal to almost exclusively social.
- *Leadership changed* from gifted and called servants to professionals.
- *Growth changed* from multiplication to addition.
- *Missions changed* from being to supporting missionaries.
- *Confession changed* from public before a small group to private in the confessional.
- *Discipleship changed* from on-the-job to classroom training.
- *Fellowship changed* from in-depth in community living to more surface in large meetings.
- *Body life changed* from lifestyle to membership.
- *Gifts changed* from edification to entertainment or extinction.
- *Empowerment changed* from God's power to man's ability.
- *Buildings changed* from functional to sacred meeting places.

• *Administration changed* from integrated to compartmental.
• *Membership changed* from producer to consumer.
• *Child-care changed* from parental to church responsibility.
• *Bible study changed* from doers of the Word to hearers of the Word.
• *Evangelism changed* from "go structures" to "come structures."

The transition from groups to buildings completed in the fourth century changed the face of the church for the next seventeen centuries. All of the above changes have continued to impact negatively upon the church as we know it. Could the way we are the church today have more to do with what happened in the fourth century at the hand of Constantine than with what happened in the first century at the hand of Jesus? Many searching Christians are beginning to suspect just that!

5
TERESA, AN APOCALYPTIC PARADIGM

This one lifetime is the center of history with as much happening in it as in all the previous lifetimes put together.
—Alvin Toffler

O ur church met Teresa through a member, trained by a community agency to sponsor at risk families. The state Child Protective Services had given Teresa temporary responsibility for seven of her grandchildren, ages two through nine. Her daughter, the children's biological mother, was in her late twenties, on drugs and supporting her habit through prostitution. Like thousands of others, through the utopia of drugs, she was trying desperately to escape her own personal hell.

The family had a history of child abuse and neglect. The two oldest daughters had recently been sexually abused by their stepfather, who was in jail, awaiting trial. Their father was in prison in Mexico for murder. All of these beautiful children, five girls and two boys, were born into a deadly social whirlpool threatening to gradually suck them under.

As I observed this situation, I saw the multiplication of evil at work. One young mother had already produced seven children who potentially would be just like her. (The men in the situation were equally or more responsible, but typically were not around.) Even if one or two of these precious children were to escape, the situation still represented a rapid acceleration of misery, pain, sin, and hurt. Multiply this situation by thousands of "Teresas" in the world and the extent of human suffering and evil comes into terrible focus. Evil abounds. Human misery multiplies.

DYSTOPIA: THE DISEASE OF THE TWENTY-FIRST CENTURY

A recent *U.S. News & World Report* article describes what is happening to Teresa, to her daughter, her grandchildren and throughout the world as "dystopia,"[1] which is the opposite of utopia. It is a situation, says Webster, "in which conditions and the quality of life are dreadful." Clearly, a large percentage of the world's inhabitants today experience a dreadful quality of life. The utopian optimism of past decades has burst like a hard boil and a dark depressing dystopia has settled like a festering sore upon the world. We are in a dangerous social cycle that threatens civilization. Even in affluent North America, this sickness has incubated in cities and is spreading like an epidemic into every segment of society. Dystopia is a worldwide sickness.

Those with no biblical understanding of man's inherently sinful nature are constantly surprised by the emergence of the dreadful conditions of dystopia. The world doesn't have a clue to its source or a solution for it. Unfortunately, even though the traditional church sympathizes with those in dystopia, it has lost an effective means through which to significantly touch the hurting in the world.

Dystopia is often associated in literature with the Four Horsemen of the Apocalypse—War, Famine, Pestilence, and Death. These terrible horsemen appear in every generation. In our century, images of dystopia flock before us in these words: "Holocaust," "Hiroshima," "Killing Fields" and "Bosnia." "Rwanda" is the latest apocalyptic word but will not be the last before this book is finished.

In Africa, we have seen the Four Horsemen of the Apocalypse thunder across the land. First came war with its accompanying death. Then came famine and death, and pestilence as the refugees fled from the war and famine into camps where cholera and other diseases took their toll. With each changing phase, death remains the one constant.

Terrible pictures have emerged out of this march of death—babes crying at the corpses of their dead mothers, mothers weeping over the still forms of skeleton children. One gut wrenching picture shows a vulture waiting beside the emaciated form of a dying child alone in the dust of Somalia.

Four important historical factors contribute to the dystopia of the world today and make up the historical context of the church as it approaches the twenty-first century—population explosion, urban implosion, social alienation, and church isolation. This is Teresa's world, an apocalyptic paradigm that threatens to destroy civilization as we know it.

THE POPULATION EXPLOSION

Statistics tell us the total number of people who have lived and died since the beginning of time approximates the total number of people who are alive today. World population in Jesus' time equaled the U.S. population today. By Martin Luther's time, the population had doubled. It took 1500 years for that to happen. In 1800, the population again doubled in only 300 years. In 1930, the population again doubled in only 130 years. From 1930-2000 A.D., the population will explode to 6.5 billion—in 70 years. The population is projected to double to 10-12 billion people sometime in the twenty-first century. The graph below will help us grasp this.

According to the United Nations Population Division, every year the equivalent of a Mexico is added to the world's population. This means that, in addition to all those who die, 90-100 million persons are added.

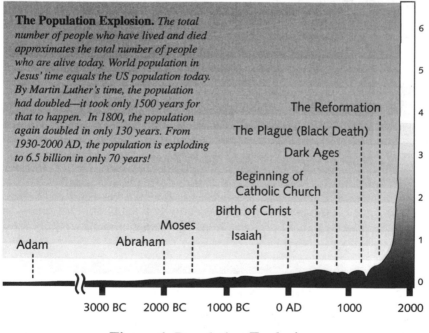

Figure 1. Population Explosion

Paul Erlich, author of the best-selling 1968 book, *The Population Bomb*, said that the current world population of 5.5 billion will double by the middle of the twenty-first century. In 1992, he said, "We were overly optimistic. When the book was written, we were adding 70 million people a year. Now we are adding 93 million a year."[2] This means the world's population will increase by the total population of the country of China (one billion plus) during each of the next six decades.

Urban Implosion

At the same time the population explosion marks this era as a dividing point in world history, urbanization adds another foreboding exclamation point. The key events of the twenty-first century are taking place in an urban context.

Statistician David B. Barrett describes different types of cities that are rising out of the population explosion. These are megacities which have reached or passed the size of one million inhabitants. By 1900 there were twenty megacities. This number grew to 276 megacities by 1985, "with future numbers estimated by the UN at 433 by AD 2000, and as high as 652 cities of one million by AD 2025."

Along with megacities, there is the rise and explosion of supercities which have populations of four million or over. "London was the first supercity, in 1870; today there are thirty-eight supercities, with 144 anticipated by AD 2025, and 220 by AD 2050."

Barrett also classifies the volcanic eruption of urban supergiants, which have populations of ten million or more. "The first supergiant was New York in 1935, the second, Tokyo, in 1958. Suddenly supergiants erupted everywhere. By AD 2000 some twenty-four urban supergiants will have risen and by AD 2050 as many as eighty."[3]

People are imploding into cities and the greater pressure and stress of city-life. Life is no longer as simple as running a small store or raising a few crops. The size alone of the population centers creates a complexity never before encountered.

Social Alienation

Sociologists call the third contributing factor to modern dystopia the "cocooning" of society. This phrase describes how people walk out of their secure office buildings into self-contained garages, get into their air conditioned cars, drive home insulated by tinted windows and soft music, turn into their driveways, push their automatic garage door openers and enter their homes, their cocoons. This is another way to describe modern man's withdrawal from society into a safe environment.

The wall or fence is one of the most revealing cocooning symbols of the city. It tells us about the psyche of the city-dweller. At the end of his drive home each day, the city dweller retreats behind walls. Barriers are built to keep the city at bay. Significant amounts of time, money and materials are used in the city just to build walls, fences and barriers that can physically separate the "we" group from the "they" groups. These walls symbolize isolation, loneliness, and fear.

Why do these physical and relational walls exist in the city? The city dweller obviously feels vulnerable, insecure and threatened by his urban environment. He cannot absorb all the complexity and change that accompanies megacities, supercities and supergiants. The walls are an answer to his physical and emotional self-preservation.

Society is out of control and real fear fills the urban jungles. The urban dweller is cut off from well-defined cultural relationships. They are denied the safety of home and family because of divorce and are expected to interact more and more with impersonal machines and computers. They are forced to endure the pain and agony of human misery and man's inhumanity to man verified in living color nightly on television. He feels his privacy is threatened even in the sanctuary of his home as he is assaulted and invaded with telemarketing, advertising, and doses of every kind of television religion known to man.

CHURCH ISOLATION

To explain the fourth factor of dystopia, I refer again to current world statistics. David Barrett uses them to argue that today is different from the past several centuries because of a rising "non-Christian" or "anti-Christian" climate. Between AD 1400 to 1700, all the world's five largest cities were non-Christian and even anti-Christian capitals. By the year 1900, all of the world's five largest cities had become strongholds of Christian life, discipleship, urban evangelism, urban missions, foreign missions and global mission.

But by 1985, two of the five cities were non-Christian, and by AD 2000, three of the top five will be cities hostile to Christian missions. By AD 2050, four of the top five will be non-Christian and anti-Christian giants of around forty million inhabitants each, in order of size—Shanghai, Beijing, Bombay, and Calcutta.

Christians within the cities have been decreasing as a percentage of urban dwellers. In contrast to the favorable urban situation in 1900, we now find huge non-Christian supercities, blocking Christian advance.

Huge cities of ten million inhabitants with no cultural roots in Christianity are erupting across the globe including Tokyo, Shanghai, Beijing, Calcutta, Osaka, Bombay. Next to follow before AD 2000 will be seven Islamic supergiants which are Jakarta, Cairo, Baghdad, Istanbul, Teheran and Karachi.[4]

Sacrificial Christianity has never been a popular choice. With these world-wide changes, the church will have to weigh the cost of confessing Christ, much less sacrificing and reaching out to those within areas where there is radical persecution of Christians.

WHAT ABOUT THE TWENTY-FIRST CENTURY CHURCH?

While the population multiplies and people implode into cities, walls are being built and Christianity is becoming more and more isolated. The church is declining as a total percentage of the population. It has lost its effectiveness to reach out to those in dystopia. I am aware of many respected statisticians who argue that church membership is increasing in relation to population. The variable is how we define "church member." If this includes children and those identified with the church in a cultural sense, then the conclusions of these statisticians may be accurate.

However, if church member means an adult actively involved in the life of the church as a "believer," we come up with a much lower figure. Most church statisticians readily admit the difficulty in obtaining a figure for believer because it carries such subjective and theological connotations. Protestant denominations can't even agree on one definition among themselves. A common definition which would fit both Catholic and Protestant would be even more impossible.

A pastor, with whom I served more than twenty years ago, clearly understood the difference in church statistics. When asked his church membership he would reply, "Do you want my *bragging* membership, or my *working* membership?"

The categories of members and believers affect our conclusions about the state of the church, which in turn affects the kinds of church strategies we develop. The cultural statistics reflecting members may have some validity, however it is the statistic of believer which truly reflects church growth. For the development of church strategies, I am more interested in identifying the worldwide working membership of the church rather than the bragging membership.

Numbers notwithstanding, the problem of strategy boils down to the difference between addition and multiplication. The population multiplies while most churches depend on strategies which result in addition or zero growth. Even the most creative traditional churches in North America use strategies that only *add* members, while the population is growing by *multiplication*. The many dynamic churches scattered across the world that use cells as their basic Christian communities are the primary exceptions to these church growth patterns.

In light of these demographic indicators, some questions come to mind. Does God know there's a population explosion? Does God love the billions being born today as much as the millions born during the day of Jesus? Certainly He does, but what is He going to do about it? Is the one-winged church the only hope for the billions of people who will be born on earth over the next five or six decades? Does God have another plan? Even the most optimistic church leaders are lost as to how the one-day-a-week church paradigm can significantly impact the population explosion!

TAG! YOU'RE IT!

Population explosion, urban implosion, social alienation, and church isolation puts us in an apocalyptic paradigm, a framework for disaster, misery and evil. What can be done?

We must ask, "Can a church isolated in buildings and dependent upon strategies of growth through additions hope to prevail against these apocalyptic forces?" Whether the church of Jesus Christ will prevail is not the question. Jesus' church has faced apocalyptic forces before and grown in spite of it. The question concerns the survival of the institutional church (Constantine's church) as we know it. Can the Sunday dominated, one-day-a-week church prosper in such a hostile and changing world without a major overhaul of how it operates?

If you and I do not ask these questions, who will? Well meaning politicians can assign governmental funds to their problems but cannot give what is missing in society which is spiritual values and power. Many "Larrys" are too disillusioned and distracted by the old paradigm to deal with the confrontations that accompany these questions. "Eddie," the consumer church member, is part of the problem and too comfortable and immature to even know there is a problem. Denominational experts are digging deeper and deeper in the same historical hole, trying to "fine tune" the traditional church. "Teresa" is drowning in her own apocalyptic whirlpool and taking her children and children's children down with her. She will never find a solution to cure her own dystopia.

That leaves you and me to come to grips with the world in which we are living. We must find a way to live in God's "holy (apocalyptic) history" so His Kingdom might be "done on earth as it is in heaven."

What will the church be willing to do in order to become God's instrument of redemption for the world we live in? Will the church die to its respectability? To its programs? To its intellectualism? To its historical denominational organizations? To its buildings? To its professional leaders who do everything for it?

Apocalyptic times call for apocalyptic measures, in the church and in our own life. We are talking about major paradigm shifts. We must begin to live out the most powerful paradigm that man has ever encountered: *The incarnation paradigm.* The incarnation paradigm may be defined as God living in history, in His church, in living resurrected presence, mighty power and eternal purpose. To enter that paradigm, we must move from present church patterns and become two-winged churches that have a hope and a practical strategy to turn Eddie into a producer, get the pressure off of Larry, and touch Teresa and her grandchildren. That is the only paradigm that can redeem the church and thereby redeem society.

If you and I won't do it, then it won't be done!

Tag! You're it!

6

TWO-WINGED CHURCH QUESTIONS

*Speed is useful only if you are going
in the right direction.*
—*Joel A. Barker*

B y now, you probably have questions about the cell church and what I and other proponents believe about it. Most people do. In this chapter, I want to address eight questions often asked about the cell church. To a certain extent, my answers in this chapter may help you understand what I am *not* saying.

Question 1: *"Are you saying the traditional church is totally wrong?"*
Absolutely not! The church as we know it isn't insincere or wrong. The traditional church is not incorrigible; *it is incomplete.* It only flaps its large group wing. The traditional church is not dead; it is crippled. The intent of this book is not to weaken the large group wing of the traditional church, but to begin to use the small group wing as well. Traditional large group life must be balanced with small group community life.
Elton Trueblood makes a case that the church must engage in both realism and idealism. The modern church's great gains as well as great losses must be considered. He suggests, however, that it is more profitable to stress the losses because it leads to change:

What we must say is not that the condition of the Church is worse than it was—which may or may not be true—but rather that the Church is far weaker right now than it might be. Areas could be occupied which are now neglected; resources could be employed which are now wasted. The real problem before us is not whether our faith has declined, but how it can be made more truly relevant to contemporary life and its urgent needs. However good the contemporary Church is, it is not good enough; it is not so good as it might be, in view of its glorious founding and in view of its current unexploited resources. And its adversaries are strong.[1]

Walking on a hill in central India, missionary E. Stanley Jones came upon a fort guarded by soldiers in ancient colorful uniforms. The fort was at one time relevant as the center of a feudal state. It once held the authority and power of the state within its four thick walls. Over time, the center and power of the state had moved beyond those walls to the city in the valley below. The fort was now high and dry, and irrelevant, with soldiers pompously guarding it.

Commenting on the story, Jones had the following to say. "That, the critics say, is the picture of the church of today. It is high and dry . . . and irrelevant. It is not geared into problems of the secular city. It is pompously guarding irrelevant values and issues."[2]

Jones recognizes the difference between the irrelevancy of values and the irrelevancy of structures and forms:

The values which the church is guarding are not valueless, and they are not irrelevant. They are the most precious values in human society today or any day. Those values may be covered up in irrelevant forms and archaic language; but stripped of those irrelevant forms and language, they are the most relevant and precious and valuable possessions ever granted to the human race.[3]

How tragic is the picture of the church today! It still possesses the most precious message and values but is too often ignored because the message and values are covered up in irrelevant forms and archaic language.

Church values are not the problem, neither is theology. The problem is the lack of a viable design through which the values and theology can be lived out. This is where the cell church movement steps in.

Question 2: *"Are you saying small groups or cells will cure everything wrong in the church?"*

Certainly not! The cell group isn't some kind of magical structure which revolutionizes the church just because of its physical properties. Without life, structures, whether of the large or small variety, are lifeless bones. When I use the word "small group" or "cell," I never mean just the physical structure. It also includes the dynamic of life within it that can only come from Christ.

The dynamic at work in a cell group is different from what happens in a large gathering, or within me as an individual. The facets of community are personal intimacy, accessibility and availability, physical contact, communication, care and help, accountability, relationship, conversation, unity, focus, and group ministry. They can't be duplicated in the same way and intensity in a large group or in the life of one individual.

Cell groups are essential to the church because of these qualities, not because of the small group structure itself. There is nothing inherently spiritual about two or three people meeting together. People get together all the time in social, political, business, religious, educational and even criminal small groups, like gangs. What is different in New Testament groups is "Christ is in the midst;" therefore the group becomes His spiritual body.

The unique aspects essential to successful life in Christ cannot be accomplished without small groups. The traditional church has tried to do that and be "church" without a viable New Testament cell unit for years. Some even see the Sunday School as fulfilling this requirement for cell group life. However, a typical Sunday School class does not live out the characteristics of New Testament cell group community. A Sunday School class is hindered by its limited time frame of one hour a week, its narrow purpose of cognitive Bible study, and the place of meeting which is isolated from life in the real world.

The qualities and characteristics of spiritual community are best expressed today as in the first century through small home groups. That is why Jesus carefully wove small groups into the basic fabric of the New Testament church. It is not the structure; it is the dynamic life of Christ Himself released in and through the small groups that makes the small group essential to the church.

Question 3: *"Does this mean the lives of individual church members in the traditional church are devalued?"*

Not at all! It is not my desire to impugn the spirituality, sincerity, or sacrifice of thousands of wonderful Christians who faithfully serve in the traditional church. They are my parents and grandparents, friends and fellow church members. Calling for a return to the New Testament church design does not question the spiritual maturity of traditional church members.

Christians can grow personally in their spiritual lives in the one-winged design. They have personal devotionals, are personal soul-winners, faithfully and systematically have personal Bible study, personally strive to be Christ-like in actions, and maintain a deep personal prayer life. The driving force behind life in the traditional church context is *personal.* Because of the *personal* rather than *corporate* nature of this kind of Christian living, it can happen in any kind or size of church structure.

The question is can I function in a New Testament way without cell group community? Granted, I can have a personal relationship with Christ and with others without cell group community. I can also participate in large group activities and worship without cell group community. But, without cell groups, it is difficult, if not impossible, to participate in New Testament community life.

To say there is more than personal or large group experiences is not to say what we have had is totally bad. Rather, it is a desire to bring to the church the blessing of experiencing Christ in community in the powerful way we see in the pages of the New Testament.

Question 4: *"Are you implying this kind of church happens quickly or easily?"*

Absolutely not! Jesus clearly understood this would not be easy. The picture Jesus gave of His church is one storming the gates of hell. Such words do not lend themselves to expectations of ease and comfort. The process necessary to become a cell church requires an incredible amount of commitment and faith.

Jesus said, "I will *build* my church." Building is a process. It took Jesus three and a half years to complete the first church. Those years were characterized by opposition, misunderstanding by His leaders, abandonment by some followers, betrayal by others, and finally death on the cross. Part III of this book paints a realistic and biblical picture about starting a new cell church and transitioning a traditional church into cell life.

Question 5: *"Why make an issue about the size of the group? Isn't the fact we meet Christ the real point?"*

God is omnipresent and can manifest Himself to thousands of people individually all at the same time. Therefore, there is no problem relating in large numbers of people to God. Neither is the problem with individuals relating to Him. I can experience God personally in a crowd of thousands. The problem is the lack of community. Because I am not omnipresent, I cannot experience community in a group of thousands as I do in a cell group. Just as I am limited physically by time and space, I am limited relationally by the number of people I can relate to in depth.

The formula for group communication lines is N x N - (N) = CL. "N" stands for the number of persons and "CL" represents communication lines. The number of persons present, multiplied by the number of persons present, minus the number of persons present, equals the number of communication lines in the group. For example, suppose four persons get together for a meeting. How many lines of communication will be present? Using the formula, we have this: 4 x 4 - (4) = CL. 4 times 4 equals 16. 16 minus 4 equals 12. In a group of four there are 12 lines of communication.

What about a group of eight people? The number of people in the group is doubled. Does that mean the communication lines also double? Use the formula. 8 x 8 - (8) = 56. There are 56 lines of communication in a group of eight. The communication lines did not just double but increased exponentially from 12 to 56.

Now what about a group of twelve? 12 x 12 - (12) = 132. In a group of twelve, for everyone to relate to the other members in some kind of personal way, there must be 132 separate incidents of relationship. Do you see why Jesus only had twelve disciples. Size of the group does make a difference in relationships and community.[4]

Jesus did not say, "Where two or three hundred or two or three thousand have gathered together, I am in their midst." It wasn't by accident or without forethought that Jesus defined the kind of group in which he would uniquely indwell by saying, "For where *two or three* have gathered together in my name, there I am in their midst" (Matthew 18:20).

The nature of community limits the size of meetings. Christians in the New Testament desired fellowship, therefore they lived together in small groups. The key factor is whether community is a goal of the church today.

Question 6: *"Isn't it oversimplification to claim one church structure is the only church structure? Don't we see several kinds of churches in the New Testament?"*

The design of the church in the New Testament was the "whole church" and the "home church." Leadership styles, methods of decision making and types of organizations appear adaptable in the New Testament, changing as they are described through the Gospels, the book of Acts and the Epistles. However, the *basic design* of the New Testament church never changes in the New Testament. At no point did Paul and the other writers indicate the church was to cease meeting in the pattern established during the early days of the church, both in homes and as the gathered church. Robert Banks says it this way:

> . . . Paul never retracted his understanding of how the church should operate. He never moved away from his view that the church is a genuine extended family in favor of a less personal, more institutional entity. He never suggested that the local church should occupy itself with only one aspect of activity—the allegedly "religious"—and only one aspect of the personality— the so-called "spiritual." He never lessened his belief in mutual ministry and shared authority for one based more on liturgical order and hierarchical leadership.[5]

Looking through our one-winged lens, we see a confusing array of "churches" in the New Testament. Through the eyes of history, these structural differences have become even more pronounced in the minds of theologians and pastors. However, only one church *design* was operating in the New Testament.

Despite adaptations, the church design remained basically the same. For example, birds are designed with two wings in order to fly. *That is their design.* Flight is their function. The flight design does not change, but the flight function may be adapted. Birds such as eagles and hawks soar and glide. Quails and turkeys fly in short bursts of energy. Swallows and other smaller birds dart as they catch insects. Hummingbirds hover by beating their little wings at unbelievable speeds. Geese and ducks fly in formation with smooth and powerful motions in their own flying functions. All are based on the same basic flying design—two wings.

In the New Testament, the basic design of large and small groups is the same. In the early church, we are not seeing many different *kinds* of "churches" but the *application* of the one church design. Unfortunately, the traditional church just hasn't made adaptations to the New Testament design of the church, it has changed the design itself by forsaking the small group community wing.

Question 7: *"Weren't cell groups simply the way people in the first century culture related? Must it be the same now?"*

In 1991, I watched a pastor struggle with the choice between the New Testament church design and the historical structure of the church. John's church (not his real name) was the largest within his denomination in a small Northeastern state. Consequently, he felt a burden to be a model for other new and smaller churches in the area. He desired to see the work grow which was not happening with the traditional approach. Somehow he came into contact with Ralph Neighbour's book, *Where Do We Go From Here?* and called about the cell church movement.

In the beginning, he was honestly exploring both the structural and theological implications of the cell church. The question he faced was, "If the concepts and principles about the cell church are New Testament, then what does that mean for my church, and for me?"

As we talked over a period of several weeks, I sensed he was feeling more and more threatened by what this approach would mean to his traditional church and personal ministry. He was gradually moving from a theological to a historical rationale of the church. Finally, after several phone conversations, he clearly stated the conclusion with which he was willing to live: "What they did in the New Testament in meeting in home groups was just the way they did it then. This is the way we do it today." In other words, he concluded the small group design of the church is primarily cultural.

The only way he could intellectually escape the contradiction between the structure of his traditional church and the New Testament church was to confine the New Testament Two-Winged approach to the pages of the New Testament. He fit the New Testament into his traditional paradigm. I hurt for that pastor because he had chosen the historical church over the church of the New Testament.

Biblical scholarship has established an impressive body of evidence supporting small or cell groups as a primary function of the New Testament church (See chapter 10). In light of all the evidence about small groups in the New Testament church, why is there still debate on the issue? The question in the minds of many is not about what happened in the New Testament. Instead, they view small groups in the church today as a basic structure that is actually unessential.

People must buy the lie that the large group and small group rhythm of the New Testament church is only a setting in life, just the way they did it then. The design of the New Testament church is placed in the same category as past cultural practices such as "greeting the brethren with a holy kiss."

If we buy this reasoning, the church today is not bound by the basic New Testament design of large groups and small groups. Church structure is at the mercy of changing historical factors and cultural convenience and becomes a product of history rather than of New Testament theology. The message of the New Testament is best lived out through the first century New Testament design of the church.

Question 8: *"Will cell churches work in the USA, Western Europe, Canada, etc.?"* You fill in the country.

I have heard this same question asked about a dozen or more countries. The tone of the question implies cell groups will not work in that particular country, that cells are a Third World phenomenon not suitable for Western culture. (Christians in Asian, African and South American countries ask the same question.)

A friend sat across the table from me and said it straight out with feeling and conviction. "Cells won't work in America!" He was a leader in denominational missions and had contributed outstanding service in starting new churches for several decades. He added, "The only way to build churches in America is through the Sunday School."

Later on (isn't it always like that?), I thought of several clever responses: "Ask Jane Fonda if cells and small groups will work in America. She is making a killing on small group aerobics classes." Or, "Ask the New Age movement if small groups will work in America. They are organizing for small group experiences everywhere." Or, "Ask innovative business leaders if small groups work in America. Business is organizing as quickly as possible into effective small working units in order to compete with the Japanese."

I could have also pointed out that one kind of small group is universal. This small group is present in every culture, society, country and every generation since the beginning of mankind. We see evidences of it in cities and jungles, rich and poor cultures, third world and advanced countries. *It is the family.* The family small group unit may vary in different cultures and parts of the world, but we can still recognize it as *family*. The very fabric of society is based upon a small group.

Probably nothing I could have said would have changed my friend's mind because he simply didn't believe in any kind of small group except Sunday School. "Believing is seeing." Of course, this is just the opposite of our normal way of saying, "Seeing is believing." We "see" only after we "believe." My friend could not "see" small groups because he did not "believe" in small groups.

The truth is that America is in the midst of a small group revolution and has been for the past several decades. Professor of Sociology at Princeton, Robert Wuthnow in his *Christianity Today* article "How Small Groups Are Transforming Our Lives," painted the broad scope of small group activity in America.

> At present, four out of every ten Americans belong to a small group that meets regularly and provides caring and support for its members. These are not simply informal gatherings of neighbors and friends, but organized groups: Sunday-school classes, Bible-study groups, Alcoholics Anonymous and other 12-step groups, singles groups, book discussion clubs, sports and hobby groups, and political or civic groups.[6]

Small groups abound by the thousands! That should be encouraging news to society in general and to the church in particular. Small groups are beneficial as a social unit. Small groups can furnish a framework for emotional therapy, life support systems, social interaction, fellowship, task accomplishments and even religious experiences. George Gallup, Jr. links small groups to societal changes. "If the sixties represented the 'Movement Decade,'" he notes, "the seventies the 'Me Decade,' and the eighties the 'Empty Eighties,' then perhaps the nineties will become known as the 'Decade of Healing.'" Gallup believes such a label is appropriate in view of the millions of Americans who have joined small, nurturing care groups seeking help for psychological, physical, emotional, or spiritual problems.[7]

7
THE BENEFITS OF THE TWO-WINGED CHURCH

*It is neither the place nor the setting nor the ritual
that is miraculous; it is the fellowship.*
—Elton Trueblood

The burning question in the government the year before the United States entered World War II was what to do about the German submarine fleet. The German Wolfpack was playing havoc with America's attempt to supply the Allied effort in Europe. Hundreds of supply ships were being sunk while crossing the Atlantic Ocean. An admiral one day declared he had the answer. "Heat the Atlantic Ocean to boiling. Then all the submarines will have to surface, and we can destroy them."

When asked how this was to be done the Admiral replied indignantly, "I gave you the idea, it's up to you to furnish the details."

President Franklin D. Roosevelt is reported to have used the above story to point out that an idea is useless if the details for doing it are so far fetched the idea is impossible. Few people will get on board with an idea that is as impractical and outlandish as "boiling the Atlantic Ocean."

The cell church paradigm must be practical enough to solve the problems associated with the old way of being church; otherwise the idea will be dismissed out of hand. Unfortunately, some believe those talking about this new way of being the church are suggesting we "boil the Atlantic Ocean."

THE "BETTER MOUSE TRAP"

New ways of thinking are never automatically adopted. Significant changes are only made after weighing the benefit of the change. Is the new idea better than the old? Do the new methods work better than the old? Is this "new thing" really a "better mouse trap?"

During this "pre-paradigm" period the old and new ideas are competing with each other for adherents. The new idea will only be accepted when it gives some kind of proof it can "solve the problems that have led the old one to a crisis."[1]

No matter how clear the vision, most people only enter into significant change which offers some practical benefit over their present methods. The cell church paradigm is not only a good idea, it is also beneficial and workable. It solves many of the problems we have struggled with over the years. However, no paradigm answers all of the facts, especially in the beginning. "To be accepted as a paradigm, a theory must seem better than its competitors, but it need not, and in fact never does, explain all the facts with which it can be confronted."[2] The cell church solution is being considered all across the world today because it shows evidence that it can actually solve the problems confronting the church.

In this chapter, I want to sum up some of the benefits of being a cell church. God supports the vision He gives with enough practical evidence to move us along to implementation, but never enough proof to destroy our need for exercising faith.

BENEFIT #1: THE CHURCH CAN SING THE MELODY!

The New Testament church sang a beautiful song with melody (small groups) and harmony (large groups). That musical score was rearranged by the fourth century. Today, the musical arrangement lacks the *melody* notes. Beautiful buildings, large crowds on Sunday, moving worship services, and impressive programs are part of the large group harmony, with very little small group melody. Consequently, no matter how loud the volume, beautiful the setting, spacious the music hall, diverse the instruments, gifted the conductor and entertaining the star performer, the sound lacks the simple and pure melody of the New Testament church. The harmony is complete only when played with the melody.

Today, those in the traditional church are forced to sing the song of the church inside the church building on Sunday. If churches sing harmony without the melody, the song will never sound like the New Testament music. On the other hand, the cell church can sing the beautiful incarnation song, both melody and harmony.

BENEFIT #2: EFFECTIVE MANAGEABLE UNITS

Armies are organized into manageable units appropriate for accomplishing the basic task. The most basic unit is the squad, which is made up of nine to twelve enlisted men. This unit makes the difference in battle. All larger groupings of soldiers such as platoons and companies exist to support and reinforce these basic fighting units. Five to fifteen Christians are the basic unit of the church. These are "God squads."

The cell unit is manageable because it is self-contained. Every task of the church can be implemented through this one basic unit. Discipleship, leadership training, evangelism, worship, ministry, fellowship and Bible study function within the basic cell unit.

It is manageable because of its size. Jesus knew the optimum size of a functioning unit when He chose His twelve. When a group exceeds twelve, effectiveness in communication and production diminishes.

This basic Christian community is manageable because of its simple assignment. The basic Christian community focuses on Christ, and is empowered and directed by Him for internal edification and external evangelism. A cell needs no special props, materials or funds. Its assignment can be accomplished by its members living in community with each other.

The cell is manageable because of its place of meeting. The cell needs no specially designed or expensive housing. Cells meet in the homes of members and can easily solve any problems related to a meeting place.

The cell is manageable because of its simple leadership structure. With a cell leader and intern the ratio of leaders to members assures proper care and development of the cell. The next generation of leaders are developed through on-the-job training within the cell itself.

BENEFIT #3: A "DELIVERY SYSTEM" ON THE "FRONT LINES"

Several years ago a picture of a particular period of Sunday church would flash in my mind each time I attended church. The time frame was not of Sunday School, congregational singing, the time of preaching, offering or invitation.

The recurring picture was the ten-to-fifteen minutes following the service, when the people left the building, got into their cars and drove out of the church parking lot. God was tapping me on my shoulder and saying, "Look at this time in the schedule of the church on Sunday. It is important! What do you see?"

In the beginning, all I saw was people getting in their cars and going home after the Sunday service. What was the big deal about church members leaving the church parking lot? "Lord, they're just leaving church and going home."

Eventually God revealed His point to me through some disturbing questions that accompanied this parking lot scene:

- Can this church still be the church, beyond the church parking lot?
- Does this church have any effective structure that operates as the church beyond the church property?
- Must unbelievers and the hurting wait until next Sunday before the church can minister to them as His living body?
- Must all these Christians now become individual "Lone Rangers" and "spiritual commandos" who are cut off from their support base and supply lines?

If a church cannot be the church beyond the church parking lot, it is not His kind of church. A church is more than what happens inside a building on one day of the week. Basic Christian community is a way for the flock to be "fed" and "tended" out in the world. It is a "delivery system" by which Christians are nurtured and unbelievers are reached with the gospel.

A major benefit of the cell church is the presence of groups out on the "front lines." The flock has ready access to fellow believers who know them, care for them and pray for them. Every member has a spiritual family that loves them out in the real world.

BENEFIT #4: CHURCH GROWTH

"The Lord added" and "the church multiplied" are phrases used in the book of Acts to describe New Testament church growth. Within several generations, a good portion of the world was either Christian or directly influenced by Christian concepts. For decades, the church has tried to replicate the multiplication seen in the New Testament.

Several programs have been tried over the years; however, none have approached first century exponential multiplication. Discipleship, mass media, institutions, and Sunday School have been touted as *the* answer for church growth, but all have fallen far short of New Testament growth.

Discipleship should result in exponential multiplication, but it hasn't. Certainly church and para-church organizations have tried, but they have failed because their strategy is only partial. What do you do with new believers when they are won? Where do they see Christian community modeled? How are those won developed to be part of the solution instead of part of the problem? Developing reproducing disciples can't be successful apart from community.

Great hope was placed in mass media over the past several decades. The expectation was every person on the face of the earth could hear the gospel. Exponential response was promised. This has not happened, and it will not. Mass media can be a voice, but that is all. It lacks the heart of the gospel which is incarnation. Unbelievers don't just need a voice, they need someone to love them and model the Christian life for them in community.

Some evidently have felt institutions would cause growth. Build schools, hospitals, seminaries, orphanages and bookstores to reach the world. Such institutions have done many good things. However, we have learned by now such institutions are more effective in maintaining the institution than sparking exponential multiplication.

Will Sunday School cause exponential multiplication? It hasn't to this point and it won't. Not because it is a bad program, but because it is set up as an informational system instead of a transformational system. If the Sunday School is the key to multiplication it would have already done it. Great amounts of time, money, personnel and materials have been assigned to Sunday Schools over the past century, and good things have come as a result. However, during the time the Sunday School has been the linchpin program of the traditional church, the church hasn't experienced exponential multiplication.

The key for New Testament multiplication of the church is the *cell unit*. The same dynamic cell growth patterns observed in a living body hold true for the spiritual body of Christ. All other schemes may contribute to addition growth, but only the multiplication of cells will result in exponential multiplication of the church. What is unique about the New Testament cell structure that creates exponential multiplication?

1. The cell structure contains all of the other structures, such as discipleship, evangelism, and bible study, within its nature and essence.
2. Growth takes place at the most basic level, the cell group.
3. Cells naturally multiply—they don't depend upon outside factors to stimulate growth.
4. Multiplication can happen in many environments, both favorable and unfavorable.
5. The cell works everywhere—it will multiply in every type of culture.
6. All necessary leaders are produced exponentially within the basic task.

BENEFIT #5: GOD'S CALLED LEADERS HAVE A PLACE TO LEAD

This is one of the greatest benefits of the cell church. All leaders called by God for the important task of nurturing the sheep and tending the lambs have a context in which their ministry can be expressed. Every leader chosen by God has a place of service worthy of God's call upon their life. God's call to be a Two-Winged leader is once again matched up with a Two-Winged structure.

Modern churches are full of frustrated men and women who have an unfulfilled ministry "call" upon their lives. Sometimes young people "surrender to preach" or talk to their pastor about "entering the ministry." Usually after considering the meaning of being an administrative pastor they, with relief, decide it was all a mistake and get on with their lives.

Others have a sense of special call later in life. They may give up their job to go to seminary or Bible school, but quickly decide what they are studying doesn't apply to what they felt called to do in the first place. So they drop out of school, go back to their home church and become "good laymen," teach Sunday school or serve in leadership positions on committees and boards. Many end up feeling they have "failed" God in some way.

These leaders are, without a doubt, set aside by God for a unique leadership ministry. Unfortunately, without the New Testament cell design, the spiritual call of most leaders cannot be fulfilled in the traditional church structure. What a waste! God touches them, and there is no place to live out what God has spoken into their lives.

My grandfather lived to be ninety-six years of age. Stewart Beckham was a Baptist deacon for more than sixty years, teaching a large men's Bible class for much of that time. Past ninety years of age, Pa was in charge of his church's extension department, ministering to the elderly in his church. He faithfully visited every Saturday with his pastor. He was a "soul-winner" and an "amening" Baptist who sat on the front pew encouraging the preacher.

I remember sitting in the swing on his front porch talking about everything from politics to heaven. One day he shared he felt God had called him to preach when he was a young man but did not respond because he had a young and growing family. He regretted not following through with that "call." His ministry in the traditional church had not completely fulfilled the call God placed in his heart.

In a New Testament cell structure, his family situation would not have eliminated him from serving in a pastoring role. He could have been like Aquila and Priscilla, leading cell groups of neighbors, or supervising a cluster of home cells, or eventually becoming a pastor of a congregation. It is tragic that the traditional church does away with the leadership role that is most productive and effective in nurturing, discipling, witnessing and ministering.

Benefit #6: The Hurts and Needs of the World Can be Touched

In a cell church every member is a minister. Therefore, personal and group ministries touch the lives of hurting people. Because the basic Christian community takes place out in the world, Christians can identify and react to real needs. Cells are healing units at the cutting edge of hurts.

The makeup of a cell church encourages personal ministry instead of relying upon professional ministry. The traditional church ministers through a staff of ministers who are paid to do certain tasks for the rest of the congregation. This severely limits the kind, number, and nature of ministries that can be implemented. For every new ministry, a team of concerned and committed Christians must be gathered, funded, administered, and supported by the church. When I pastored a traditional church, I felt "God's arms were shortened," and He could not respond to the real hurts and needs in the world apart from elaborate and expensive social programs.

On the other hand, the design of a cell church provides a framework of cells already out in the world that can serve as support for personal ministries. Cells out on the "cutting edge" are able to identify needs, fund those ministry needs and personally respond.

BENEFIT #7: EXPERIENCING CELEBRATION WORSHIP

During the time I pastored my third church, I developed a splitting headache every Sunday. Eventually I traced this recurring pain back to its source. I was so uptight about what happened on Sunday morning that anxiety was manifesting itself in real pain. The performance demands upon me as a pastor were the source of my headache.

Trying to drag unprepared Christians into the presence of God for worship is enough to give any man a headache. When I recognized the source and turned loose of it, the ache left my head, but not my heart. I continued to long for an experience of genuine worship where prepared Christians participated in worship from an overflow of God's presence, power and purpose.

Is there a type of worship which isn't worked up, promoted, produced, or performed? Can a pastor ever hope to look out across a congregation on Sunday and see members ready to worship without the use of human motivation or entertainment? How can genuine heartfelt worship naturally express itself with the right amount of emotion and reverence?

The cell church structure offers hope this can happen. Members who have experienced the intimate presence of Christ in cell group life will be drawn by His Spirit to celebrate the goodness and greatness of God together in large groups. Then genuine heartfelt worship naturally expresses itself with the right amount of emotion and reverence. This kind of worship is so powerful, orderly, spiritual, and genuine that an unbeliever will be struck by the presence of God. Large group worship provides a setting for inspiration, information, revelation and celebration. Small group community allows application, edification, incarnation and preparation.

Those experiencing true worship while celebrating God's greatness will be drawn back into the experience of God's love within warm, intimate cell meetings. This is the rhythm of worship between cell and celebration that is possible in the cell church.

BENEFIT #8: SPIRITUAL GIFTS CAN BE PROPERLY EXERCISED

On a given Sunday, in one-winged churches across the world, two "gift" scenarios play themselves out. In the first one, the gifts of the Spirit are not a part of what is happening in worship or during the week. There is no expectancy of experiencing either the real presence and power of Christ or an excitement beyond human experience. In scenario number two, every gift of the Spirit necessary to prove the credibility of God is exercised during Sunday worship. The pastor, with the help of a few professional leaders, uses the gifts of prophecy, interpretation, discernment, working of miracles, healing, speaking in tongues, and other expected manifestations of the Spirit.

Are these two extremes the only alternatives? Operating within a one-winged structure, exercising spiritual gifts is severely limited because there is only one context in which to express them: celebration worship.

A cell church structure, on the other hand, gives a New Testament context in which spiritual gifts can operate in a natural and genuine New Testament setting. Who is tempted to "show off" in a small group setting? If someone fails to exercise a gift in the proper way, that person can be admonished in a loving and personal manner. The scriptural expectation that *everyone* will exercise spiritual gifts is possible only in the cell group setting. Leaders are now released from the requirement of exercising the gifts for the entire body.

BENEFIT #9: THE BUILDING PROBLEM IS NEUTRALIZED

In the cell church, buildings no longer shape the church; the church shapes the buildings. This does not mean cell churches will not have buildings. They will. However, in a cell church, buildings will have a better chance of being functional, rather than sacred. The church building will not be so important that it becomes the "church," rather than the place for church assembly. Traditional churches build in order to grow. Cell churches grow and then build.

Donald A. McGavran, writing about the benefits of house churches for early Christians, notes that "at one stroke they overcame four obstacles to growth." Three of these obstacles listed by McGavran are related to a building in one way or another:

Obstacle 1: Building costs that would divert resources away from ministry and witness.
Obstacle 2: A fixation on the synagogue that would hinder movement into Gentile communities.
Obstacle 3: Introversion that would prevent Christian homes from being evangelistic centers.
Obstacle 4: Limited leadership that would restrict spiritual leadership to professionals.[3]

Earnest Loosley said:

How would the church have met the present and ever changing situations today, had it never built church buildings? Is not the answer this: she would have developed and extended the idea of "house-churches," encouraging groups of neighbors to meet in one another's homes, to share in group fellowship. A large part of the problems confronting us today cannot be solved within our traditional practice of erecting places of worship. We must set ourselves to thinking along other lines.[4]

Howard Snyder puts it this way:

In these days, so parallel to New Testament times, the traditional church building is an anachronism the church can no longer afford. This is not to say no community of believers should ever hold property. But it is to say that any property, any building, should be held lightly, and should be an expression of a clear biblical understanding of the true nature of the church. Any building so held must be functional—a means, not an end. The road back to the Middle Ages is all too easy to take.[5]

BENEFIT #10: THE CELL CHURCH INTEGRATES MINISTRY

Small groups allow the church to have an integrated rather than compartmentalized approach to ministry. Howard Snyder suggests small groups integrate the work and ministry of the church when viewed in three areas:

1. Psychological integration
2. Sociological integration
3. Theological and biblical integration

Viewed psychologically, small group structures enable "the integration of the cognitive, affective and volitional aspects of human behavior." The small group gives a context in which the whole person can experience the presence, power and purpose of Christ in daily living.

Viewed sociologically, these structures enable and stimulate "the primary, face-to-face relationships which give the church social cohesion and power." The church has a delivery system in society where both the believer and unbeliever can experience healing in community.

Viewed theologically and biblically, these structures provide "the context for experiencing the fellowship of the Holy Spirit and the convicting, correcting, discerning, and encouraging work of the Spirit and the Word." (2 Timothy. 3:16; Hebrews. 4:12). In other words, the "ecclesiola structures (small groups) provide spiritual integration."[6]

In addition to Snyder's three areas of integration, the cell church also integrates the church *organizationally*. Jesus designed the New Testament church to function as a simple integrated system organized around life in small group cells. We have developed a compartmentalized complex administrative system organized around independent programs.

The result is a system that demands more and more administration, promotion, buildings, activities and money. This approach also takes a heavy toll upon those who are required to run it. The compartmentalized system always hangs precariously on the edge of collapse, exuding complexity and defying focused and simple solutions. Greater and greater effort is required on the part of leaders to keep it running.

The complexity of the church grows out of the design of the church. A Two-Winged bird is a thing of simplicity and beauty when it flies. A one-winged bird trying to fly is all motion, energy and activity, and it gets nowhere.

The "spinning plate act" is a perfect illustration of this phenomenon. A performer, usually with an assistant, spins a plate on top of a long thin rod. He keeps adding more rods and plates, depending upon centrifugal force to keep the plates perched upright on top of the rods.

This is programmed disaster, because as the plates spin more slowly, they are in danger of falling. The performer must run back and forth between the plates giving a fresh spin. The audience gets involved by encouraging the performer, pointing out plates about to fall and expressing dismay when a plate breaks.

As a church leader, I have felt like that performer. I got my row of spinning programs in the air, only to realize very quickly that the more I got in the air, the harder I was working to keep them all up. Very soon I found myself making a mad dash back and forth between all of the compartmentalized programs, furiously working to keep everything in the air. I soon learned that the problem is not in my lack of effort or skill. The problem is that each plate must have its own source of power to keep spinning. If I could operate one source of spinning power for all the plates, my job would be relatively easy.

The church was never designed by Christ to work this way. Jesus designed a simple integrated cell system, not a complex compartmentalized program system. When we get tired of running, we may want to try church Jesus' way!

PART II

FOUNDATIONS FOR A SECOND REFORMATION

For thus says the high and exalted One
Who lives forever, whose name is Holy,
"I dwell on a high and holy place,
And also with the contrite and lowly of spirit
In order to revive the spirit of the lowly
And to revive the heart of the contrite."
—Isaiah 57:15

8

CHURCH STRUCTURE REFLECTS GOD'S NATURE

"Am I a God who is near," declares the Lord, "And
not a God far off? Can a man hide himself in hiding
places, So I do not see Him?" declares the Lord.
"Do not I fill the heavens and the earth?"
declares the Lord.
—Jeremiah 23:23-24

C ell churches have incredible potential to meet the ever growing needs of a desperate society. We have seen in Part 1 that this structure of basic Christian communities has innate advantages over other structures. However, the advantage of the cell church is found in theology, not structure. The two-winged church reflects the nature of God in His transcendence (greatness) and immanence (closeness). This serves as a theological paradigm for the church. J. I. Packer explains transcendence and immanence:

> God is not limited. He is eternal, infinite, and almighty. He has us in His hands; but we never have Him in ours. Like us He is personal, but unlike us He is *great*. In all its constant stress on the reality of God's personal concern for His people, and on the gentleness, tenderness, sympathy, patience, and yearning compassion that He shows toward them, the Bible never lets us lose sight of His majesty, and His unlimited dominion over all His creatures.[1]

Transcendence describes the nature of God as above and different from man, even unapproachable. Transcendence means divine reality is not limited to our natural order but is above it. God is the "most high" God.

On the other hand, immanence expresses the indwelling of the Divine in the world. God is the "most nigh" God. Immanence explains God's nature as close and near. This definition of transcendence and immanence can also be interpreted as follows:

• Transcendence: How man relates to God in His Godness.
• Immanence: How God relates to man in his humanness.

In discussing the divine goodness of God, C. S. Lewis recognized the uniqueness of the transcendent and immanent relationship between God and man:

> God is both further from us, and nearer to us, than any other being. He is further from us because the sheer difference between that which has Its principle of being in Itself and that to which being is communicated is one compared with which the difference between an archangel and a worm is quite insignificant. He makes, we are made: He is original, we derivative. But at the same time, and for the same reason, the intimacy between God and even the meanest creature is closer than any that creatures can attain with one another. Our life is, at every moment, supplied by Him: our tiny, miraculous power of free will only operates on bodies which His continual energy keeps in existence—our very power to think is His power communicated to us.[2]

Figure 2 contrasts words often related to God's transcendence and immanence. These words show God's relationship to man and man's relationship to God.

Over the centuries, fierce theological battles have been fought at the point of the related doctrines of the transcendence and immanence of God. As is the case with many doctrinal disagreements, this seems to have been a problem of balancing two equally true and important truths about the nature of God. The pendulum has swung back and forth between the extremes of transcendence and immanence. God is "wholly other," and also "indwelling and abiding in the midst."

In this book, I don't want to rehash the details of past theological battles. My goal is to apply the balanced biblical doctrine of the tran-

Figure 2. Transcendence and Immanence Scale

scendence and immanence of God to ecclesiology, the doctrine of the church. If God is both transcendent and immanent, what does that mean about the theology and structure of the church?

Howard Snyder suggests large group corporate worship and small group *koinonia* are necessary for man to encounter God as He really is:

> Believers need those times of solemn corporate worship in which the High and Holy God is honored with dignity and reverence. But in the midst of the dignity and reverence many a lonely believer inwardly cries out for the warm, healing touch of *koinonia*. Believers need to know by experience that the Most High God is also the Most Nigh God (Is. 57:15). If traditional corporate worship is not regularly supplemented with informal opportunities for *koinonia*, believers easily drift into a practical deism while the church becomes the sacred guardian of a powerless form of godliness. On the other hand, form and liturgy take on new meaning for Christians who are living and growing in *koinonia*.[3]

This is not a debate about structure, but a truth about how God chooses to be His body on earth, express Himself to mankind, and operate His Kingdom in the world. In relation to mankind, God has chosen to be both transcendent (far), and immanent (near)—this is His theological paradigm. Let us explore the Old Testament for some of the exciting moments when God reveals Himself to His people in His transcendence and immanence.

ADAM AND EVE: LIVING WITH THE TRANSCENDENT AND IMMANENT GOD

In Genesis one, the transcendent and eternal God, separate from and above all creation, spoke the world into existence with a word. Then in Genesis 3:8, we observe God walking in the midst of the garden seeking Adam and Eve in what looks like a regular appointment. The Creator's special walks are a lovely picture of a caring and Fatherly relationship. Was this relationship primarily transcendent or immanent, or both at the same time? Could it be that before the fall, Adam and Eve related to God in a way lost through the fall, experiencing both His transcendent and immanent nature at the same time? Could it be that in the fall, man lost the capacity to experience God in His full nature, but most of all, in His close companionship?

In whatever way God related to Adam and Eve in the beginning, we know it was Satan's objective to spoil that special relationship. In the very first temptation, the serpent began to worm his way between God and Adam and Eve. Satan sought to isolate man from the immanence (closeness) of God by questioning the truthfulness of God, a key element in any relationship. Then Satan attacked God's transcendent (all-powerful) nature by questioning His sovereign right over Adam and Eve and all of creation.

Satan destroyed man's special relationship with God so Adam and Eve would be left alienated from God, each other and the world around them. Genesis tells us they sinned, hid from God in the garden and were forced to flee from this special relationship of transcendence and immanence.

ABRAHAM'S "VISITORS"

Even though Adam and Eve severed their special relationship of transcendent greatness and immanent closeness, God did not stop revealing

Himself to mankind. God directed Abraham to leave the land of Ur, the "cradle of civilization," and to journey toward a chosen land and a special destiny. Abraham's early encounters with God seem to be more transcendent than immanent in nature.

At the age of ninety-nine, the Lord appeared to Abraham in a unique encounter, reaffirming the promise of a descendent (Genesis 18). During this intriguing appearance, which was either one event or two events taking place within the same general time, Sarah laughed. In a human sense, it was laughable to her that they would produce an offspring at their age, even if God Himself promised it.

However, at the Oaks of Mamre, three visitors reaffirmed to Abraham (as Sarah listened in the tent) that the covenant would be fulfilled by the birth of a son. Many consider this appearance of God to Abraham to be a special physical manifestation of God, or a *theophany*. Whatever one calls it, it was definitely a life changing "near presence" experience for Abraham and Sarah with the immanent God.

MOSES ENCOUNTERS "I AM"

God called Moses to return to Egypt and deliver the children of Israel at the burning bush (Exodus 3 and 4). This unusual personal and intimate revelation of God to Moses had a profound influence upon his life. God revealed His name to Moses as "I AM" and gave authority to Moses in that name. The verb used for the name of God means "to be actively present"[4] and could be translated as Living Presence. The name given to Moses to identify the transcendent God reveals Him to be immanent.

In contrast, on Mt. Sinai (Exodus 19-23) God revealed Himself as the transcendent awesome God with all of the smoke, thunder and lightening. On the mountain, Moses came into the transcendent presence of God. The children of Israel were restrained by boundary markers surrounding the mountain where the transcendent God revealed Himself and His commandments to Moses.

THE PILLAR OF CLOUD AND THE TENT OF MEETING

God led the children of Israel away from Egypt toward the Promised Land with a cloud by day and a pillar of fire by night. The Lord promised Moses, "My Presence will go with you." God guided them, yet at a distance and in a form appropriate for the transcendent God.

In these chapters, we learn of another meeting place between Moses and God somewhat like the burning bush, but different from the encounter on the mountain or the pillar of cloud. In Exodus 33 and 34, God met Moses at the Tent of Meeting. ". . . whenever Moses entered the tent, the pillar of cloud would descend and stand at the entrance of the tent, and the Lord would speak with Moses. . . . the Lord would speak to Moses face to face, just as a man speaks to his friend" (Exodus 33:9-11). This is an immanent (close) encounter between God and Moses.

This was also a group encounter, different from that solitary meeting of Moses with God at the burning bush. The passage says the people would go into the tent of meeting as well, and Joshua, Moses' military aide, did not leave the tent. No wonder Joshua became such a great leader. From the very beginning, he experienced God in His immanent closeness just like Moses.

While God spoke to Moses "face to face, as a man speaks with his friend," Moses said, ". . . show me Thy glory" (Exodus 33:18). God said to Moses,

> You cannot see My face, for no one may see Me and live!" The the Lord said, "Behold, there is a place by Me, and you shall stand there on a rock; and it will come about, while My glory is passing by, that I will put you in the cleft of the rock and cover you with My hand until I have passed by. Then I will take My hand away and you shall see My back, but My face shall not be seen (Exodus 33:20-23).

The face of God is mentioned in both encounters. However, there is obviously a difference between God speaking to Moses face to face in the tent of meeting and Moses seeing the face of God on Mt. Sinai. Why can Moses meet God face to face at the tent of meeting and yet not live if he sees God's face (glory) on the mountain?

The difference is God in His naked transcendence (greatness) and God in His revealed immanence (closeness). The transcendent God is beyond the comprehension and humanness of created man. God in His transcendence is always on the mountain, above us and beyond us. No mortal man may see the face of God in His transcendence and live.

God also revealed Himself in His immanence so He could speak to Moses "face to face, as a man speaks with his friend." God met Moses at the burning bush, at the tent of meeting, and when Moses carried the tablets of the commandments, "the Lord came down in the cloud and stood there with him and proclaimed his name, the Lord." This is not a contradiction in terms, but a truth of the nature of God, who relates to man in both transcendent greatness and immanent closeness.

Man knows God in "a mediated immediacy." The incarnation is God's supreme expression of God's transcendent deity in immanent human context. God "emptied Himself." Whatever that phrase means, it implies God presented Himself in such a way to man that His greatness and sovereignty did not hinder His closeness. God's "wholly otherness" from man did not forbid His becoming like man. God's immanent expressions of Himself in the Old Testament foreshadow the incarnation.

God in Christ established the tent of meeting upon earth, not just for a special leader like Moses and not just in a special place. Jesus' tent of meeting upon earth was not restricted to priests who could enter the Holy Place, or to the High Priest who entered once a year to the Holy of Holies to meet God with sacrifices for the sins of the people.

Through the incarnation, every Christian has become a tent of meeting where God is "face to face, as a man speaks with his friend." Every Christian is the temple of God, the dwelling place of God. In addition, when two or three Christians come together in His name, they enter into the tent of meeting of God where God speaks to them "face to face, as a man speaks with his friend."

JOB: FROM THIRD PERSON TO FIRST PERSON DIALOGUE WITH GOD

The early part of the book of Job records his tragic suffering and pain. The reactions and comfort of his four friends represent the prevailing teachings on suffering. We can also learn something about the transcendence and immanence of God from Job's ordeal.

From the beginning scene of the book, God appears to be transcendent in the heavens, observing all that is happening down below. The events of Job's life were set into motion out of a dialogue between God and Satan, far away in a transcendent place. Both Job and the friends addressed God and talked about Him with transcendent awe. They talked about God in the third person. Job cried out:

Oh that I knew where I might find Him,
That I might come to His seat!

I would present my case before Him
And fill my mouth with arguments. . . .
Behold, I go forward but He is not there,
And backward, but I cannot perceive Him;
When He acts on the left, I cannot behold Him;
He turns on the right, I cannot see Him. . . .
Therefore, I would be dismayed at His presence;
When I consider, I am terrified of Him (Job 23:3-4; 23:8-9; 23:15).

Job's friends may have had faulty views of the cause of pain and suffering, but they did have lofty insights into the transcendence of God. Their view of God was summed up by Elihu, the youngest and last speaker, who declared: "The Almighty—we cannot find Him; He is exalted in power;" (Job 37:23).

The early chapters of Job reveal God in third person transcendence. However, in the conclusion of the book, God suddenly breaks upon the scene in a powerful and immanent revelation of Himself. Beginning with chapter 38, God spoke to Job for more than four chapters in a first person dialogue—they talked up close and personal. Gone was Job's complaint that He couldn't find God or that God was silent. All of a sudden God was too close for comfort.

God did not answer Job from afar but drew near to answer the more fundamental question about His immanence. God did not explain Job's pain and suffering but rather revealed His nature. The manifestation of God in nearness, while not answering all questions about pain and suffering, at least put them in proper perspective.

The essence of God's answer is that the transcendent God is not obligated to answer His created beings or to explain the circumstances of life. Man has no right to demand explanations from the Creator. But, while explaining His transcendent nature to Job, God spoke to Job in a personal way out of His immanence.

This is the great mystery of God. He is transcendent (great and beyond man), but teaches man about that transcendence from His immanence (nearness). The "most high" God explains who He is in His unapproachable transcendence by becoming the "most nigh" God.

This close and personal experience with the most nigh God caused Job to respond in Job 42:5-6: "I have heard of Thee by the hearing of the ear; But now my eye sees Thee; Therefore I retract, And I repent in dust and ashes."

DAVID KNEW THE IMMANENT GOD

Psalm 23 speaks to man's heart because it reveals the immanent and caring Shepherd. David knew God in His greatness and transcendence as is evident in other Psalms. David also knew God in His close, immanent nature. That is why this Psalm of David is so special to us today. The Shepherd God is with us (immanent) in every place of life:

"in green pastures"
"beside quiet waters"
"in paths of righteousness"
"through the valley of the shadow of death"
"in the presence of my enemies."

"Thou art with me!" That is a statement of one to whom God has revealed Himself in a "most near" relationship—in His immanence. What is the personal result of this intimate relationship with God?

"I shall not want."
"He restores my soul."
"I fear no evil."
"You comfort me."
"You prepare a table for me."
"You anoint my head with oil."
"My cup overflows."
"Goodness and mercy will follow me all the days of my life."
"I will dwell in the house of the Lord forever."

ELIJAH: EXPERIENCING GOD ON MT. CARMEL AND MT. HOREB

The prophets had a special relationship with God which was unique to their calling. Their job was to deliver messages from the transcendent God. However, God seemed to reveal those transcendent messages with immanent (most nigh) communication. To pagans, God might send messages by handwriting on a wall, but to the prophets, God spoke often in ways that revealed His immanent nature. We see these two characteristics of God's relationship with the prophets in the life of Elijah.

God orchestrated a contest with 400 prophets of Baal (I Kings 18 and 19) on Mt Carmel, with the blue Mediterranean as a backdrop. Fire, one of the sacred elements of this pagan religion, fell from heaven and consumed the altar and sacrifice prepared by Elijah. God was triumphant, and the 400 prophets of Baal were killed. Then out of fear and desperation Elijah ran from Jezebel into the desert. Finally God ministered to him under the juniper tree and spoke to Elijah at the mouth of the cave on Mt. Horeb. God was very near in a "still small voice." Again we see the personal attention of God who ministers to Elijah and speaks to him out of His immanent (close) nature.

YAHWEH AND EMMANUEL

The name Yahweh expresses the transcendent nature of God and the name Emmanuel expresses His immanent nature. Yahweh was the sacred name of God to the Jews that was too holy to even pronounce. When they returned from the Babylonian exile, the Jews more and more sought to protect the name of God from what they considered to be irreverent familiarity. The divine name was represented by the four consonants JHWH (JHVH).

The word meant, "he that is" or "he that is present" and implied God was ready to manifest himself as helper. Even the transcendent name of God carried with it a hint of the immanence of God who was near enough to help.

Emmanuel, God with us, is the name designated for the Messiah. "For a child will be born to us, a son will be given to us; And the government will rest on His shoulders; And His name will be called Wonderful Counselor, Mighty God, Eternal Father, Prince of Peace" (Isaiah 9:6). This One will be God in our midst: divine and living immanence. The incarnation is ultimate immanence. God once again walks in the garden, but this time in the physical form of the children of Adam and Eve.

THE TEMPLE DESIGN

A final way the Old Testament reveals God's nature is seen in temple worship and its ceremonies and festivals. Temple worship was primarily directed upward toward the transcendent God. But God had also provided a way in the design of the temple to teach the truth of His immanent nature. Within the Holy of Holies the Shekinah of God, "I Am," Jehovah, Yahweh resided in the midst of the temple.

God was in the midst of the temple, as in the camp, however He was made inaccessible and unapproachable to the ordinary Jew by a graduated access system which became more and more restrictive as one neared the Holy of Holies. The immanent God was hidden within the temple's transcendent structure.

The conception was of a Holy of Holies at the center of a series of concentric rectangles arranged according to a decreasing scale of sanctity as they became farther removed from the most holy place. This symbolism of degrees of sanctity was repeated in the persons of those who were allowed access to the several courts. Gentiles were at the greatest distance, then Jewish women, then Jewish men, then priests and finally the High Priest in the Holy of Holies. This holiness was also maintained in the materials of which the Temple buildings were constructed; the more precious materials were closer to the Holy of Holies.

This may be one of the most difficult relationships a people can have with their God. God is near in the place of worship, but unapproachable. God resided in the midst of His people in the Holy of Holies, but was inaccessible and completely cut off from personal encounter and communication with them. Only once a year, and then only after careful ceremonial cleansing, the High Priest ventured through the barriers into the presence of the "most nigh" God.

This encounter was so uncertain and fearful that tradition says a rope was tied to one foot of the High Priest to pull him out of the Holy of Holies if he were struck down by being in the presence of God. A "near presence" experience with God was a "near death" experience as far as the Hebrews were concerned.

The death of Jesus forever changed the place of the Holy of Holies of God. Jesus in the flesh was the incarnation of the "most high" God brought "nigh." At the moment of His death on the cross, the thick veil of separation in the Holy of Holies was torn asunder from top to bottom, from God down to man, and man began to experience God in a new way. Age old barriers were removed between God and man. God became the most "nigh" God living in his people and abiding in the midst of his *ecclesia*.

9

THE TRANSCENDENCE AND IMMANENCE OF CHRIST

... in Christ we find the union of the immanent
and transcendent.
—E. Y. Mullins

T hroughout the pages of the Old Testament, God expressed Himself to the patriarchs, Kings and prophets in both transcendence and immanence. For more than 2000 years God was to His people the transcendent God as a normal occurrence and the immanent God on special occasions to chosen men.

Jesus came to show the Father: "I manifested Thy name to the men whom Thou gavest Me out of the world" (John 17:6). Could Jesus reveal the Father without revealing His transcendent and immanent nature? Certainly not! Therefore, in the fullness of time, Christ manifested Himself to and through His church as the transcendent and immanent God. What in the past was only occasional and for special persons became the norm for all followers of Christ.

"For truly I say to you, that many prophets and righteous men desired to see what you see, and did not see it; and to hear what you hear, and did not hear it" (Matthew 13:17).

The Patriarchs and Prophets in the Old Testament had rare encounters with the transcendent and immanent nature of God. Today these encounters become the norm in the incarnate Christ and in the new spiritual body (the *ecclesia*). Jesus designs His church to experience and live out both the transcendent and immanent nature of God. Francis Schaeffer said it this way:

> Christians are to demonstrate God's character, which is a moral demonstration, but it is not only to be a demonstration of moral principles; it is a demonstration of his being, his existence.[1]

JESUS CLAIMED TRANSCENDENT AND IMMANENT DEITY

Jesus' discourses in John 13-17 give the most extensive explanation of His relationship to His followers. John 14 is also an astonishing claim of deity by Jesus.

He explains how He will continue to relate to His disciples within the full nature of God after He ascends to heaven. Jesus will return to the Father in heaven and will sit at the right hand of God on the throne which is His rightful position. He is the eternally transcendent God. In heaven He will prepare a place for His followers that, "where He is, they may be" (John 14:1,2).

Later in this chapter, Jesus teaches He is the immanent Christ on earth. Through the Holy Spirit, Jesus will also be with His disciples on earth in an immanent way. He is preparing a place for His followers on earth that "where they are He may be" (John 14:16-18). That place is His church. He is the eternal living incarnation within His body, the church.

In this passage, only God is transcendent and immanent in the way Jesus is talking about Himself. God is the only "most high" God, and God is the only "most nigh" God! There is no other like Him in heaven and on earth. Jesus claims for Himself the nature of God as He explains the design of His church.

Francis Schaeffer makes a case that Christ will be with the church in a unique way "between the ascension and Second Coming." Speaking of John 14:16-18, Schaeffer concludes that "the raised and glorified Christ will be with the church through the agency of the Holy Spirit." He elaborates on the meaning of this:

> Notice the words "I will not leave you orphans, I will come to you." The promise of Christ—crucified, risen, ascended, glorified—is that he will be with his Church, between the ascension and his second coming, through the agency of the indwelling Holy Spirit.

These are universal promises, made to the Church for our entire era. These are the things that the world should see when they look upon the Church—something that they cannot possibly explain away. The Church should be committed to the practical reality of these things, not merely assenting to them.[2]

WHO IS WITH ME IN THIS WORLD?

It is obvious from the disciple's questions and Jesus' answers in John 14 that the disciples were concerned about His leaving. "Don't be troubled. You believe in God, believe also in me."

They are confused about how He will relate to them in the future. Will He be transcendent or immanent, remaining in their midst in some form or residing with the Father in heaven? How will He relate to the Father who is the most high God? How will He show Himself to His disciples? What will be the relationship between the Father, Son and Spirit to the Christians who remain on earth? How can He be in heaven "at the right hand of the Father" and also on earth "in their midst?" How will Jesus relate to Christians between the ascension and the second coming?

These were their questions and the reason for their anxiety. Jesus attempted to explain the mystery of His new relationship with His church and to calm their fears. These questions about Jesus' relationship with us individually and corporately are important for the church to consider today.

First, Jesus explained the Spirit would be with them (John 14:16-17). "And I will ask the Father, and He will give you another Helper, that He may be with you forever; that is the Spirit of truth, whom the world cannot receive, because it does not behold Him or know Him, but you know Him because He abides with you, and will be in you." He then expanded on that explanation by talking about His own relationship to them. "I (Jesus) will not leave you orphans. I (Jesus) will come to you!" (John 14:18).

After explaining the Spirit would be on earth with His followers, why then does Jesus confuse the issue by making the clear claim that He would also be with them? The issue becomes even more perplexing when He later explains the Father will send the Spirit and then declares, "We will come to him, and make Our abode with him" (John 14:23). So the Father is both in heaven "sending the Spirit" and here on earth "abiding" with the disciples with Christ.

I can see how the Spirit is with me, but what do Jesus' other teachings mean about the Father also abiding with me and Jesus Himself coming to me? Who is down here with me and in what form?

This same ambivalence is present in Romans 8:9-11 where Paul explains how God relates to the believer on earth. Paul interchanges the Father, Son and Spirit when explaining how God indwells. In verse nine, Paul states that the Spirit lives in me: "You, however, are controlled not by the sinful nature but by the Spirit, if the *Spirit of God* lives in you" (NIV). In verse ten, Paul switches to Christ in me. "But if *Christ is in you*." Then in verse 11 Paul says, "And if the *Spirit of him* who raised Jesus from the dead is living in you . . ." Who raised Jesus from the dead by his Spirit? Whoever raised Christ from the dead also lives in me by the Spirit. That is God, the Father, who lives in me. It is evident Paul is not writing for clarity about the Trinity but for reality.

Who is down here with me? The answer: God in His full nature is here with me. God in His full Trinitarian expression becomes alive in the New Testament design of the church. All three persons of the Godhead participate in Christ's spiritual body on earth. Jesus' theological paradigm of the church gives a way to understand the space/time riddle about who is down here on earth with me. God has made provision to relate to me in three special ways:

- Within the large group setting of the "whole body"
- Personally
- Where two-or-three are gathered in a small group meeting

The large group setting gives a context in which the focus can be upon the "most high" God in the heavens. In that large group experience the church experiences God as Trinity. This is why the church sings:

Holy, Holy, Holy Lord God Almighty!
All Thy works shall praise Thy name, in earth, and sky, and sea;
Holy, Holy, Holy! Merciful and Mighty!
God in Three Persons, blessed Trinity!

As an individual Christian, I also experience God in Trinity. I know Christ is in me, the Father abides with me and the Spirit indwells me. That is my personal experience with God.

In John 14, Jesus carefully reveals another kind of relationship He uses to relate to His followers. This is in addition to the personal (individual) indwelling and the large group (mass) indwelling. The small group gives a special setting in which Christ will live with His disciples in every age as He did with the disciples in that first special community of twelve.

The cell group setting establishes an intimate context for experiencing the "most nigh" God in our midst. We must not forget, God always expresses Himself as the "most nigh" God in a Trinitarian way: Father, Son and Spirit.

OUR JOHN 14:20 RELATIONSHIP WITH CHRIST

Most Christians are comfortable with the teachings of "Christ in me." My experience, and probably yours as well is: Christ is in me, the Father abides in me, the Spirit is in me. Our personal relationship with God is a Trinitarian relationship.

"On that day you will realize that I am in my Father, and you are in me, and I am in you."

I (Christ) in the Father.
You in Me (Christ).
I (Christ) in you.

Praise God! This is our personal relationship with the Trinity. Sealed in this way within the Trinity we boldly ask, "What can separate us from the love of Christ?"

The picture in John 14:20 that Jesus uses to show the Christian's personal relationship to God reaches from earth to heaven. Christ is in me on earth (immanent); and I am in Christ, who is in the Father in Heaven (transcendent). In Christ, my personal relationship reaches all the way to the Father in heaven. All is well and good about the believer's *personal* relationship with Christ between the ascension and the second coming. The individual Christian is sealed in the Trinity all the way from earth to heaven.

OUR MATTHEW 18:20 RELATIONSHIP TO CHRIST

"Lone Ranger" Christianity lives in a vertical relationship to God alone. I am in Christ. My point of salvation is Christ is in me. This is the point of my sanctification. I can experience this personal relationship with God when I am alone or with crowds of hundreds or thousands. This is the believer's John 14:20 personal relationship with Christ. It is a wonderful experience.

Christ is also in the midst of His community (Ephesians 2:11-22). Living in relationship with Him within His *ecclesia* means I live in relationship with you as a Christian brother or sister.

This teaching about Christ in the midst of His church is often confusing to Christians. How does Christ relate to us when we come together in cell groups? Could it be possible for Christ to be with two or three Christians who gather in His name in a different way than just relating out from the lives of each individual Christian in the group? This is what Jesus teaches in John, and this is also my personal experience in cell groups.

Jesus assures us of a corporate indwelling as well as a personal indwelling. In the same way you and I understand Christ to be in us as individuals, we can understand Christ is in the midst of us when we gather together in His name in a small group context.

Matthew 18:20 explains my corporate relationship to Christ when I am with you and two or three other Christians. "For where two or three have gathered together in my name, there I am in their midst." The "I" here in Matthew 18:20 is the same as the "I" in John 14:20 when Jesus used the "I" to refer to Himself, the Father and also pointed to the Spirit. The "I" is also Christ.

We cannot claim Christ indwells us personally in a unique John 14:20 relationship and at the same time deny that same relationship with "two or three" as promised in Matthew 18:20. Yet that is exactly what we have done in practice. It has taken me years to understand the same Trinitarian relationship I experience personally also comes alive when I meet you and several other Christians in an encounter with Christ. In fact, it has been my experience that Christ is able to manifest Himself to me in a greater and fuller way when I am with "two or three." This means I am not sufficient in myself to receive the full revelation of Christ. To experience Christ in the fullest way, I need you and others to live with me in community. The cell meeting could be viewed as a group devotional with the Lord, while other experiences (individual and large group) are usually "personal," self-focused encounters with God.

Jesus said in John 14:18, "I will not leave you orphans, I will be with you." That is the promise of an immanent, personal, close relationship. This is a promise not only to the individual Christian but also to the

Christian community. Most of the time we experience this promise of Christ's presence in our personal relationship with God. But we feel orphaned because we do not live in the unity of His presence as a family in small group community. How sad!

Because of my personal relationship with Christ and Christ in me, as well as your relationship with Christ when we come together in His Name, we become His living body in which Christ, the Father, and the Spirit abide in the midst. This is His church in its most basic form. We experience the immanence of God in a personal relationship and in a corporate relationship. Here is a summary of how this happens:

- Several individual spiritual relationships become a common group, a spiritual entity—His body. Christ takes my personal John 14:20 relationship with Him (Christ in me. You in Me (Christ). I (Christ) in the Father) and fits it together with other Christians into a Matthew 18:20 relationship (where two or three are gathered in My name, I am in their midst). In relationship with Him, He forms us together into His spiritual body on earth.

- My personal relationship with Him and your personal relationship with Him then becomes more than the sum of our individual spiritual experiences with Him. Together we know Christ in a fuller way than we can know Him in our individual experiences.

- Together in His name we become His living body in which He indwells, empowers, and ministers.

Earnest Loosely, in *When the Church was Young*, said:

When a man met Christ—when the church was young—he was awed at the riches he received in having an indwelling Lord. *Then* he came into the *community of believers* and was awed again. The wonder of the daily fellowship, the care, the protection and "community" of the church . . . brand new creation . . . was a totally new experience for mankind. Saved men were a different species and they had a *habitat* to live in that was unique to that species. No one had ever known anything like the church . . . the community of the redeemed. Here was the *other* great magnetism of the church when she was young: Herself![3]

CHRIST'S PRESENCE WAS UNIQUE IN THE NEW TESTAMENT CHURCH

In Thailand, the necessity for Matthew 18:20 became obvious to me. Human organization, wisdom, and technique would not penetrate the darkness of centuries of Buddhism and spiritism. I had already suspected the theology of the church was more than I had either studied or experienced. Living in the midst of Buddhism for fifteen years confirmed my suspicion. God did not so much change my theology of the church as He challenged the practical meaning of my ecclesiology in day to day living. Ray Stedman added to this understanding when he wrote:

> The Church is here on earth, not to do what other groups can do, but to do what no other group or human beings can possibly do. It is here to manifest the life and power of Jesus Christ in fulfillment of the ministry which was given Him by the Father . . .[4]

Back in the United States, I began to explore the nature of this new kind of church God had placed in my heart. On several occasions, I wrote down what I understood about the nature and operation of the New Testament church. Always, in the jumble of ideas and pages of scratching, two phrases with three simple concepts would appear. "What God indwells He empowers." "What God indwells and empowers He uses."

These two phrases were a broken record in my mind. I could not escape them, and yet I couldn't find a place to put them either. Finally, in studying the nature of the cell (small group), the phrase began to make sense. At last it hit me. This was about the cell unit. God indwells and empowers His church at this most basic level! What God indwells and empowers He also uses. From this discovery came a simple acrostic that I call the three "P's:"

The *Presence* of Christ: "What He indwells."
The *Power* of Christ: "He empowers."
The *Purpose* of Christ: "What He indwells and empowers, he uses."

The meaning of Christ's indwelling presence in His church is essential for the understanding and operation of the church. Jesus designed His church to be His living, incarnate body on earth. This kind of church will only work if He makes it work. He is the source of its life, power and mission. If the church is His body, He must indwell it and give it life.

Francis Schaeffer understood that the uniqueness of Christ in the first century church must carry over into the twentieth century:

> This abiding presence of Christ gave them a sense of power, of adequacy, of readiness to cope with any situation that arose. These men were never at a loss to know the thing to do. Infinite resources of grace and wisdom and strength were available for them to draw upon . . . a reservoir in the unseen realms that could never be exhausted. Men who felt that all the resources possessed and exercised by Jesus in the days of His flesh were still waiting to be appropriated and used (John 14:12) would not shrink from any task that challenged them. Neither should we, if we had a like simple faith and confident trust and an experience with a living, reigning, indwelling Lord![5]

The abiding presence of Christ made the difference in the early church. The church today will never be like the early church until it also lives in the abiding presence. Small home groups were an important part of that dynamic first century experience. Jesus' presence with His disciples in community during His three and a half years of ministry, the groups in homes immediately after Pentecost, the continuing reliance on small group meetings in homes in the missionary work of Paul link the abiding presence of Christ with a small group design in church life.

GOD *DOES* EXPRESS HIS NATURE THROUGH STRUCTURES!

Linking God's nature to a church form is radical to some. We should not be surprised that God's revelation of Himself is expressed through appropriate forms. God has used forms and structures in the past to teach truths about Himself. Altars of sacrifice were used as special places to encounter God. The Ark of the Covenant was a form used by God to manifest Himself. So was the Tabernacle. The Tent of Meeting in the wilderness was a place of meeting God. Mt. Sinai was a sacred place. The Temple was carefully designed by God to reveal Himself. The Holy of Holies was most sacred because there God revealed Himself in a special way. In the New Testament, Jesus designed the church in a simple form of large group and small group meetings. The large group and small group settings we see operating in the New Testament provide a unique context for God to express His transcendent and immanent nature to His followers. God expresses Himself to man when he is alone and when he is in community. Within these two contexts God reveals Himself as the great eternal God and as the close intimate God.

The large group and small group settings have certain characteristics which make them better suited for the expression of either the transcendent or immanent nature of God. Of course, God can and does intermingle these two relationships and expresses transcendence in small groups and immanence in large groups. God is Sovereign and can express Himself any way He desires in any setting. Think about the directional thrust in the two meetings. In the large group, the focus most often begins with transcendence, seeing God in greatness, and moves into immanence. On the other hand, in the small group the directional focus most often flows within the circle. In the cell, Christ is in the midst of His people on earth, starting with immanence and leading into transcendence.

Jesus' purpose in His design of the church is first of all for the church to experience God in His full nature of transcendence and immanence. His second purpose is to use His church as an instrument to reveal God's transcendence and immanence to the world. Failure to use Christ's design is not a failure at the point of structure but at the critical point of theology. The church that refuses to use Jesus' simple New Testament design is not only rejecting the New Testament design of the church, but is in danger of misrepresenting the very nature of God Himself.

10

AQUILA AND PRISCILLA—
NEW TESTAMENT
COMMUNITY

There is to be an orthodoxy of community
as well as an orthodoxy of doctrine.
—Francis Schaeffer

L uke recorded that the first believers met day by day, not only in the Temple (the gathering of the whole church) but in their homes (the home congregations), eating with glad and humble hearts, praising God and enjoying the good will of the people (Acts 2:46, 5:42, 20:20). The New Testament church functioned as a fellowship in the first century within this dual context or setting. The gathered context met as the whole church, assembled as the congregation, and went to the temple. The scattered context met as home churches, joined together in cells, and went house to house.

This simple structure created a special rhythm or melody in the first century church. Howard Snyder, Elton Trueblood and Ray Stedman all use the word "rhythm" to describe the structure of the New Testament church. For example, Howard Snyder wrote:

There was always this harmonious small-group/large-group rhythm, the small group providing the intense community life which gave depth to the large-group gatherings (whether the later were for worship or for witness).[1]

Elton Trueblood stated:

Ordinarily, the rhythm of the Church is such that there should be
the establishment of the base on Sunday and the scattering during
the week, but, since there is nothing sacred about particular days,
there is no good reason why, in particular instances, this pattern
should not be reversed.[2]

Ray Stedman added:

But in the early church a kind of rhythm of life was evident in
which the Christians would gather together in homes to instruct
one another, study and pray together, and share the ministry of
spiritual gifts. Then they would go out into the world again to let
the warmth and glow of their love-filled lives overflow into spon-
taneous Christian witness that drew love-starved pagans like a
candy store draws little children.[3]

AQUILA AND PRISCILLA

Historian F. F. Bruce introduces us to a couple who were at the very
heart of the first century church. They were Mr. and Mrs. Typical
Christian Leader who lived the New Testament "rhythm" of the church.
Understanding their life in the church will help us understand the practical theology of the New Testament church. They not only held an
orthodoxy of doctrine but lived an orthodoxy of community:

Early in the year 50 an interesting Jewish couple made their way
to the synagogue in Corinth. They had lived in Rome for some
years, but lately an outburst of rioting among some of the Jews of
Rome had given the Emperor Claudius the not unwelcome
opportunity to impose restrictions on the Jewish community there
which were tantamount to their expulsion. The edict of expulsion
had no long-lasting effect; many of the Roman Jews, however,
had to find a home elsewhere for a time, and among those who
found their way to Corinth were the couple we are speaking of, a
leather worker called Aquila and his wife Prisca. Aquila was not
a Roman Jew by birth; he was born in Pontus, on the Black Sea
coast of Asia Minor. His wife—known to her friends by her more

familiar name Priscilla—seems to have belonged to a higher social class than her husband; she may have been connected with the noble Roman family called the *gens Prisca*. This couple appear to have been associated with a new movement in Judaism which had occasioned the rioting at Rome; . . .[4]

This couple was part of the ministry of Paul in Rome, Ephesus and Corinth. Not only were they friends with Paul, but they mentored Apollos as well. They knew the meaning of Christianity and the inner-workings of the New Testament church probably as well as any other first century couple. They were leaders who functioned at the most basic level of ministry. Aquila and Priscilla were home church leaders, the basic working unit of the early church. Aquila and Priscilla's church paradigm was much closer to that of the cell church than the cathedral.

The early doctrine of the church (ecclesiology) included the following elements. These factors validate the small group as the primary form of first century church life. They suggest the church today cannot function in a New Testament rhythm without Jesus' New Testament small group design:

- They met in homes.
- Worship was by participation rather than by being a spectator.
- Teachings often reflected a small group context.
- The agape meal was observed from house to house.
- Gifts were exercised in a small group (cell group) context.

MANY HOMES

Scriptures indicate first century Christians met together in homes for praise, fellowship and teaching (1 Corinthians 16:19; Romans 16:5; Colossians 4:15; Acts 5:42). Michael Green, in *Evangelism in the Early Church,* lists several homes during the first century that were used for this purpose:

- Jason's house at Thessalonica was used for this purpose.
- Titus Justus, situated provocatively opposite the synagogue (with which Paul had broken) at Corinth was a meeting place.
- Philip's house at Caesarea seems to have been a place where visit-

ing seafarers like Paul and his company as well as wandering
charismatics like Agabus were made welcome.

- Lydia's house at Philippi was both a place of meeting and a place of
  hospitality for Paul.
- Aquila and Priscilla seemed to maintain a church in their home
  wherever they lived, in Corinth or Rome.
- The Jailer's house at Philippi was used as an evangelistic center
  after his dramatic conversion.
- Stephanas' household was baptized by Paul in person and Paul
  apparently used his home "for the service of the saints."
- The upper room of a house in Jerusalem owned by the mother of
  Mark was the church's earliest known meeting place. "It is hardly
  surprising that the 'church in the house' became a crucial factor in
  the spread of the Christian faith."[5]

From time to time the early church did come together for the meeting of the whole church. Some try to prove large meeting places did not
exist prior to the fourth century. Others, who support the large church
concept quote early writings that show large synagogues and church
buildings were in use, implying the large setting was the preferred way
of the first century church to meet. In *The Large Church*, John N.
Vaughan reports:

> Eusebius alone mentions eleven occasions of the destruction of
> already existing church buildings during the reign of seven
> Roman emperors.
>   Our best records indicate that a variety of places were
> adapted by early Christians for their gatherings. These included
> homes, upper rooms, the temple, synagogues, hillsides, teaching
> halls, pagan temples, and particularly civic basilicas. Prior to the
> reign of Constantine, churches had long owned cemeteries,
> places of assembly, and all the paraphernalia of worship.[6]

Who is right? Did the early church meet in large or small meeting
places? The answer is both are right. The nature of the church is to function with two wings: the church gathered in the congregational setting and
the church scattered in the community cell setting. The problem today is
not in proving the church existed in both large congregations and small
cells during the first century. That is evident in the New Testament. Our

problem today is that the traditional church ignores the New Testament pattern and lives without New Testament community. In light of the overwhelming evidence, how can that continue?

PARTICIPATION WORSHIP

The kind of worship described in the New Testament suggests a small group setting as its primary worship context. Much of what the New Testament records about worship will not fit into the large group meeting we use today, no matter how much we try to force it. The first century Christians saw each other's faces, not just the back of the head of someone sitting in the pew in front of them. First century Christians were participants, not spectators in worship.

Paul describes their worship in the Epistles. In Ephesians 5:18-19 and the companion verses in Colossians 3:12-17, Christians are to be "filled with the Spirit, speaking to one another in psalms and hymns and spiritual songs, singing and making melody with hearts to the Lord."

This type of worship is one another worship. Worship participation was with God but also with one another. The flow of their worship was upward toward God and also horizontally, with one another. They worshiped God together, as well. First century Christians were actually involved both with God as the object of worship and with their fellow worshippers as the instruments of worship. They were not soloists in worship, but part of a choir who were together lifting worship up to God.

It also involved several tasks or activities. Psalms, hymns and spiritual songs are set into the context of all of the gifts: prophecy, words of knowledge, tongues and interpretation. Many people had to participate in this type of worship if all of these activities were to take place. This was not being done by two or three performers providing all of these activities for everyone else!

In Colossians 3:12-17, Paul creates a picture of intimate body life. This type of worship had a small group context for forgiving one another, bearing one another's burdens and being forbearing toward one another. These were small group actions, not large group activities.

Paul described a type of worship that presupposes the small group setting as an essential part of the experience. Therefore, it is extremely difficult, if not impossible, to fit the words and actions of first century worship into the one-winged church structure of the twentieth century church. Worship set in a large group context encourages a performance from the platform rather than participation from the pew. The first century Christians were not spectators cheering on the worship team, but vital players together in the important event itself.

The traditional church has tried all kinds of techniques to get the congregation involved: responsive readings, responsive answers, congregational singing, greeting one another during the service and other techniques. In the Orient, everyone may pray out loud at the same time, giving some feel of congregational participation. No matter what is tried, our worship today cannot look like, feel like or sound like first century worship. This is not because we lack their sincerity or spirituality but because we lack their structure. Paul's picture of worship in the early church can take place today using a small group church context along with the large group setting.

New Testament Teachings

All of us bring our own interpretive "glasses" (paradigms) to the Bible when we read it. These glasses help us interpret the context and setting of what we are reading. For years, I read the New Testament with my one-wing church glasses. The only way I could interpret teachings in the New Testament was to filter it back through the church of which I was a part. My church met in large impersonal groups which were led by professional religious leaders within the confines of church buildings. Some passages just did not make sense when I tried to apply them within the modern church context in which I lived.

Matthew 18:15-17 was one of those passages. Jesus' teaching about the way to reconcile personal differences is difficult to fit into the normal one-winged church structure. "And if your brother sins, go and reprove him in private; . . . But if he does not listen to you, take one or two more with you, . . . And if he refuses to listen to them, tell it to the church; and if he refuses to listen even to the church, let him be to you as a Gentile and a tax gatherer."

There seems to be too big of a jump between taking one or two with you and the next step of taking it to the church. It is overkill if one is wearing one-winged glasses, and the church refers to Sunday morning, with hundreds or thousands present. Imagine implementing this process using only the large group definition of church. How many separate cases of discipline and confession would be brought up on Sunday morning during worship among the church? This is why discipline, in most cases, is ignored in the traditional church. It is simply too disruptive and painful to practice this kind of accountability in a large worship atmosphere.

Jesus' teaching makes perfect sense when seen through Two-Winged Church glasses. The church was the small home cell group that knew the problem and the people involved. The one or two would come out of the small group itself. If the person would not be reconciled before the cell group, then severe discipline was to take place at that level. This means Jesus' teachings can apply in a natural way. Forcing Jesus' teaching into the large church setting which is our definition of church is not natural, workable or New Testament. By ignoring the small group we miss the opportunity to apply many New Testament teachings to life in a natural way, instead making application arbitrarily and artificially.

THE AGAPE MEAL

In Acts 2:46, we learn they continued "with one mind in the temple, and breaking bread from house to house, they were taking their meals together with gladness and sincerity of heart." The Lord's Supper was a small group event in the early church.

The agape meal was the remembrance meal of Christ. He began the first Lord's Supper in the upper room in the simple Jewish family format which was followed during special family occasions. Bread was broken in the beginning, and then the wine was served as a toast at the conclusion of the meal. Jesus gave spiritual meaning to a very ordinary family event. The informality and personal warmth of this meal cannot be duplicated in a large setting. The early Christians were able to remember the Lord in just the way He asked them because they had a small group context. The remembrance of His life and death, His sustaining and sacrificing, His residence with them and His redemption for them was set into an informal and simple family setting.

Today, we have no context to do what Jesus asked us to do because we only have a large group meeting. William Barclay says:

> There can be no two things more different than the celebration of the Lord's Supper in a Christian home in the first century and in a cathedral in the twentieth century. The things are so different that it is almost possible to say that they bear no relationship to each other whatsoever.[7]

The observance of the Lord's Supper in the New Testament suggests small group meetings were the primary way the church functioned.

GIFTS EXERCISED IN A SMALL GROUP

The way gifts were used offers another piece of evidence which supports the small group setting. Speaking of the use of gifts, Paul says, "When you assemble, each one has a psalm, has a teaching, has a revelation, has a tongue, has an interpretation" (1 Corinthians 14:26). He also says gifts are to be subject to the control of the church as well.

According to Paul's first letter to the Corinthians, gifts are to operate so that every one has the freedom and the opportunity to participate with a psalm, teaching, a revelation, a tongue, or an interpretation. Yet Paul also expects all of this to be done in decency and order. Where and how can the church come together so there is both the freedom and the order needed as spiritual gifts are exercised?

Only a limited number of gifts fit into the large group event meetings. This means most of the gifts spoken of in the New Testament cannot be exercised in the large group setting. Gifts of preaching, teaching or worship function in the large group setting. Also, the New Testament records the gifts of healing and miracles being exercised in large group public events. However, the large group setting simply does not meet either the criteria of freedom or order in the proper use of other spiritual gifts we see in the New Testament.

Exercising spiritual gifts only in a large group setting results in an extreme posture toward gifts of one kind or another. In the large group meeting of some churches no freedom exists for the gifts to operate at all. The formal format of worship has been carefully prepared over the years to eliminate surprises or embarrassments by the inclusion of any gifts except those exercised by trained professionals. In other large group meetings, little order exists so the gifts can edify the church as a whole. Gifts become personal activities which primarily benefit individuals exercising their personal gift within the larger body. Or, the large group format showcases the gift abilities of one or a few highly visible leaders.

How can one person be subject to prophetic oversight in the midst of a huge crowd in the way Paul is speaking? In most large services where the gifts are expected to be present, leaders either exercise all of the gifts from the platform or they are held hostage to someone exercising a gift without discernment or order from the congregation. This is the nature of a large meeting. This picture is certainly not what we see happening in the way Paul describes the use of the gifts in the New Testament.

The only context that nurtures New Testament balance, order and freedom in exercising gifts is a small group setting. In this type of group, few are tempted to play to the gallery (at least not after the first time) because no one can escape spiritual admonition if they use a gift in a carnal and unspiritual way. But freedom is also there for God's Spirit to pour out His gifts through His people.

AQUILA AND PRISCILLA IN YOUR CHURCH

If Aquila and Priscilla visited your church for a week, what would they find? Would they see the elements of life that they experienced in New Testament times? They would look for what they experienced in the first century to identify the church. Yes, the doctrine would be the same and they would surely consider this important as they looked at modern churches. But would they get invited to various homes where Christ is in the midst and relationships are developed? Would they participate in worship and see other non-leaders expressing their hearts to God? Would they enter into relationships of accountability and openness and take communion in the midst of family? Would they see all members operating in their gifts, in freedom and accountability?

They would enjoy the good teaching and large group worship, but they would also yearn to experience the life and relationships of Christ's body experiencing His presence. When they saw this also existed they would happily join in, because they would have found the kind of church they knew in the first century.

11

THE THEOLOGY OF LUTHER, SPENER, AND WESLEY

The Reformation was a revolt against papal authority
but not against the Roman concept of the church as
an institution.
—William R. Estep

T he original design of the church has surfaced in some unlikely
places and circumstances in history. Pockets of Christians have
worshiped God in the context of cell and congregation during
every period. Even some of the most famous church leaders considered
or actually implemented a cell strategy. When the church, because of
persecution, has been forced out of Jerusalem, Christians have returned to
the New Testament small group pattern.

MARTIN LUTHER'S NINETY-*SIXTH* THESIS

Martin Luther, the leader of the first Reformation, intended to reform
church structure along with church theology. Luther identified three kinds
of worship in his Preface to *The German Mass and Order of Service.*

The first, he said, is the Latin mass, and the second is the German
liturgy. Notice Luther's comments on the third kind of worship, which
sounds like the home groups of the New Testament:

These two orders of service must be used publicly, in the
churches, for all the people, among whom are many who do not
believe and are not yet Christians. . . . That is not yet a well-

ordered and organized congregation, in which Christians could be ruled according to the gospel; . . .

The third kind of service should be a truly evangelical order and should not be held in a public place for all sorts of people. But those who want to be Christians in earnest and who profess the gospel with hand and mouth should sign their names and meet alone in a house somewhere to pray, to read, to baptize, to receive the sacrament, and to do other Christian works. . . . Here one could set up a brief and neat order for baptism and the sacrament and center everything on the Word, prayer and love. . . .

In short, if one had the kind of people and persons who wanted to be Christians in earnest, the rules and regulations would soon be ready. But as yet I neither can nor desire to begin such a congregation or assembly or to make rules for it. For I have not yet the people or persons for it, nor do I see many who want it. But if I should be requested to do it and could not refuse with a good conscience, I should gladly do my part and help as best I can.[1]

Meeting in small groups in homes was Luther's unwritten theses which he believed, but failed to implement. D. M. Lloyd-Jones points out that Luther became depressed as the reformation continued. He felt that the churches which had responded to his teaching were lacking in true spiritual life and vigor. Lloyd-Jones writes:

Another thing that greatly aggravated this feeling [of depression] which developed in him was the phenomenon of Anabaptist . . . He had to admit that there was a quality of life in their churches which was absent in the churches to which he belonged. So he reacts in two ways to them; he has got to discipline his people against them, and yet he wishes to have in his church the kind of thing that was working so well in their churches. The result of all this was that he felt that the only thing to do was . . . to gather together the people who are truly Christian into a kind of inner church.[2]

Luther knew that if he reformed the doctrinal wine, he had to also reform the structural wineskin of the church. What hindered Luther from following through on this reform of church lifestyle as well as theology?

D. M. Lloyd-Jones believes it was a spirit of caution, political considerations, a lack of faith in the people in his churches, and fear of losing the movement to the Anabaptists.

What would the church look like today if Luther had been as successful in the area of structure and lifestyle as he was in the area of theology? One can only speculate, but I believe the church would be significantly different. Luther continued to use the Catholic Cathedral design as the wineskin for his new doctrines, *and it leaked.*

BETWEEN LUTHER AND WESLEY

Small groups continued to show up even after Luther decided to use the old cathedral structure. Doyle L. Young, in his insightful book *New Life for Your Church,* traces small groups within the Pietist movement. He has an excellent study of Philip Jakob Spener, the father of Pietism (1635-1705).

Dr. Young points out "as early as 1669 Spener had come to see the church's identity required Christians to meet together regularly in small groups to encourage and discipline one another." To Spener this was not "a pastoral strategy but a necessary correlate of ecclesiology." Young quotes Spener as saying:

> It is certain in any case, that we preachers cannot instruct the people from our pulpits as much as is needful unless other persons in the congregation who by God's grace have a superior knowledge of Christianity, take pains by virtue of their universal Christian priesthood, to work with and under us to correct and reform as much in their neighbors as they are able according to the measure of their gifts and their simplicity.[3]

Spener evidently began these meetings in 1670 in order to provide mutual encouragement and oversight. Spener called his groups *Collegia pietatis* (pious gatherings). The pious gatherings met twice weekly and were attended by both men and women. In the beginning, the group discussed the previous Sunday sermon or read devotional works. Later, the groups were focused on discussion of Scripture.

The results were not as Spener hoped. Dissension within some of the groups developed and opposition from the established, institutional Lutheran church with governmental backing hindered the movement. In Frankfurt, the city council refused to allow the groups to meet in homes.

Spener felt when the groups returned to the church building, they ceased speaking openly in the meetings. This was, for all practical purposes, the death of the experiment to give reformed theology a reformed structure.

THE THREAT OF THE "REAL" CHURCH

In the Pietist movement, the members of the small groups were not to consider their fellowships to be the real church when spoken of in the same breath with the institutional church. At this point, Spener may have been making a concession to the cathedral church. His theology certainly considered the small groups to be the church. However, his public statements took into account that his approach would frighten the established structure. Therefore, Spener used statements that the established status quo would find less threatening. The word church was reserved for what happened on Sunday. In so doing, Spener made small groups an appendage to the established church and doomed the movement.

Spener was a victim of an inadequate definition of his own small groups. Seen as less than the real church, they could not survive when opposition came from the traditional church, which was considered to be the real church. From his writings, we see Spener never intended for these *ecclesiolae in ecclesia* (little churches within the church) to replace the institutional church. He forbade celebration of the sacraments in the home groups. In *Pia Desideria* Spener wrote that the *Collegia* were to be:

> Instrumentalities through which the church was to be brought again
> to reflect the image of the early Christian community. . . . [They]
> were not meant to be the means to separate "true" Christians from
> others and of imbuing the former with a pharisaic self-image.[4]

I have great sympathy for Spener. Here was a man with a vision of the renewal of the lifestyle of the church of his day. He knew that reformation of theology had something to do with reformation of church form. He sought to implement what he called a "crucial biblical motif." But he ran straight into the institutional, one-day-a-week structure of his day which was protected by the government.

Consequently, Young says by 1703 (thirty-three years after the beginning of the *Collegia* or small groups), Spener had become cynical and cautious about the groups and established no others when he moved from Frankfurt. But to give him credit, Spener did attempt to implement a new structure, something Luther left only as a good theological consideration.

JOHN WESLEY'S NEW WINESKINS

Samuel Wesley, the father of John and Charles, began to lay the foundation for a kind of religious society as early as 1701-1702. Susannah Wesley, mother of John and Charles, began a home meeting which grew to such proportions that Samuel, away in his circuit riding responsibilities, became alarmed and requested her to stop the meeting. She wrote him in essence "if you desire to be in conflict with God's will, I will obey you rather than God."

John Wesley ultimately gave the shape and force to the movement. Howard Snyder, in his book *The Radical Wesley: Patterns of Church Renewal* chronicles Wesley's movement toward the church as small groups. Wesley was indeed restoring a New Testament pattern to the church of his day. Snyder writes of Wesley:

> The Methodist societies were divided into classes and bands. Perhaps it would be more accurate to say the societies were the sum total of class and band members, since the primary point of belonging was that this more intimate level of community and membership in a class was required before one could join the society. . . .
>
> The class meeting was the cornerstone of the whole edifice. The classes were in effect house churches (not classes for instruction, as the term class might suggest), meeting in the various neighborhoods where people lived. . . .
>
> The classes normally met one evening each week for an hour or so. Each person reported on his or her spiritual progress, or on particular needs or problems, and received the support and prayers of the others. "Advice or reproof was given as need required, quarrels were made up, misunderstandings removed: And after an hour or two spent in this labour of love, they concluded with prayer and thanksgiving."[5]

WESLEY AND THE TRADITIONAL CHURCH

Some traditional leaders accused Wesley of causing a schism by drawing church members into the classes. Evidently, he was accused of "gathering churches out of churches." In modern vernacular, he was accused of stealing sheep. He categorically denied this! His response was, "If you mean only gathering people out of buildings called churches, it is. But if you mean, dividing Christians from Christians, and so destroying Christian fellowship, it is not."[6]

If one is looking for the reason Wesley succeeded in establishing a cell movement where others failed, it lies in his understanding of the nature of these "classes." These small groups (classes) functioned as the church. They did what the church was supposed to do. When opposition came, Wesley was not distracted by the traditional church that considered itself to be the real church. The classes were real church to Wesley and were therefore his primary focus. They were functioning with the authority of the body of Christ. Because Wesley placed such a high spiritual purpose and doctrinal nature on his classes, they could withstand the resistance of the traditional church.

Wesley protected his small groups because he correctly identified them as the very heart of his movement. He simply would not waste his time on people if they would not meet in society. He recorded in his journal on May 26, 1759:

> I found the little society which I had joined here two years since had soon split in pieces. In the afternoon I met several of the members of the praying societies: and showed them what Christian fellowship was, and what need they had of it. About forty of them met me on Sunday, 27, in Mr. Gillies's kirk, immediately after Evening Service. I left them determined to meet Mr. Gillies weekly, at the same time and place. If this be done, I shall try to see Glasgow again: If not, I can employ my time better.[7]

Wesley summed up his attitude about the "classes" in a letter, "Those who will not meet in class cannot stay with us."[8] Wesley's major emphasis and work was to develop the church at this community level. Wesley's life shows God has always sought to restore His church to the New Testament design of small groups. George Whitefield, Wesley's contemporary and an outstanding evangelist, also understood the importance of the small groups. During the Wesleyan awakening in eighteenth century England, George Whitefield wrote to his converts:

My brethren . . . let us plainly and freely tell one another what
God has done for our souls. To this end you would do well, as
others have done, to form yourselves into little companies of four
or five each, and meet once a week to tell each other what is in
your hearts; that you may then also pray for and comfort each
other as need shall require. None but those who have experienced
it can tell the unspeakable advantages of such a union and
communion of souls. . . . None I think that truly loves his own
soul and his brethren as himself, will be shy of opening his heart,
in order to have their advice, reproof, admonition and prayers, as
occasions require. A sincere person will esteem it one of the
greatest blessings.[9]

HOW THEY FELL SHORT

Where did these efforts fail in establishing a self-perpetuating cell
church movement? Historically, small group movements have been
weakened at two points: First, leaders of traditional churches resisted a
different way of being the church and stamped out new movements.
Applying this to today, one group of modern writers on small groups
wrote, "The primary obstacle to home cell groups in the United States is
not adapting them to western culture but in overcoming the resistance to
innovation by a very tradition-bound institution."[10]

The second point of weakening was an inadequate theological understanding of the nature of small groups on the part of its proponents. With
the exception of Wesley, the leaders failed to teach that these groups were
actually the church.

Luther, Spener and Wesley correctly defined the wine of theology
and doctrine as it related to small groups. They failed at the point of either
their understanding of the traditional structures or their provision for the
groups to relate to the existing traditional structures after strong leadership was gone.

12

CHRISTIANITY FROM
THE NECK UP

*There must be something the world cannot
explain away by the world's methods, or
by applied psychology.*
—Francis A. Schaeffer

When Daniel B. Wallace's son was struck with a life threatening disease, this seminary professor learned something about the need to experience God in His nearness and vitality. In his own words, "It was this experience of my son's cancer that brought me back to my senses, that brought me back to my roots."

He speaks for multitudes within the church who struggle for life in the reality of God's personal presence and power. My heart went out to him because I have known the same dryness. What separates us from a present and caring Father? How do we end up at a place where we are going through what he calls a "purely cognitive exercise?"

In *Christianity Today,* Dr. Wallace shares the following feelings in his article entitled, *Who's Afraid of the Holy Spirit?*

> In the midst of this "summer from hell," I began to examine what had become of my faith. I found a longing to get closer to God, but found myself unable to do so through my normal means: exegesis, Scripture reading, more exegesis. I believe I had depersonalized God so much that when I really needed him I didn't know how to relate. I longed for him, but found many commu-

nity-side restrictions in my cessationist environment. I found a suffocation of the Spirit in my evangelical tradition as well as in my own heart.

The emphasis on knowledge over relationship produced in me a bibliolatry. For me as a New Testament professor, the text is my task—but I made it my God. The text became my idol. . . .

The net effect of such bibliolatry is a depersonalization of God. Eventually, we no longer relate to him. God becomes the object of our investigation rather than the Lord to whom we are subject. The vitality of our religion gets sucked out. As God gets dissected, our stance changes from "I trust in . . ." to "I believe that . . ."[1]

Dr. Wallace sums up God's work with a description of God's immanence: "In seeking God's power, I discovered his person. He is not just omnipotent; he is also the God of all comfort." We should not be surprised that we all search for spiritual meaning to life. The pain of spiritual emptiness can be found in the pew, the pulpit and the professors chair.

TWO DISTORTIONS OF GOD'S NATURE

The church of the twentieth century is now experiencing the ravages of both deism and pantheism. Deism (secular humanism) results from an extreme position on the transcendence of God. God is totally beyond man and thus cannot be experienced. The universe runs itself. Pantheism (New Age, Eastern Mysticism, the occult) takes an extreme view of the immanence of God by seeing God as part of His universe and everything as part of God. Both of these philosophies are prevalent inside and outside the church today. In one (deism/secular humanism) God is too far away. In the other (New Age pantheism) God is too close and familiar. His identity is absorbed into His own creation so the reality of God as a Person (the Person) is lost. J. Rodman Williams describes deism and pantheism this way:

Deism should be carefully distinguished from theism. Theism, unlike deism, views God as involved in the world, hence miracles may occur. Historic Christianity is theistic therefore, not deistic. Theism is about midway between deism and pantheism. Theism, like deism, emphasizes the transcendence of God, and, like pantheism, it emphasizes the immanence of God—but without the extremes of either. Deism is absolute transcendence (God totally removed from the world); pantheism is absolute immanence (God wholly identical with the world). Theism as expressed in Christian faith affirms both God's otherness and His involvement: He is Creator and Sustainer, Maker and Redeemer.[2]

Francis Schaeffer was a prophetic voice warning about the secular humanism world view that has invaded the church in the twentieth century:

Our generation is overwhelmingly naturalistic. There is an almost complete commitment to the concept of the uniformity of natural causes in a closed system. . . .

According to the biblical view, there are two parts to reality: the natural world—that which we see, normally; and the supernatural part.[3]

According to Schaeffer when we use the word supernatural, we must be careful:

The "supernatural" is really no more unusual in the universe, from the biblical viewpoint, than what we normally call the natural. The only reason we call it the supernatural part is that usually we cannot see it. That is all. From the biblical view . . . reality has two halves, like two halves of an orange. You do not have the whole orange unless you have both parts. One part is normally seen (natural), and the other is normally unseen (supernatural).[4]

How does Schaeffer's teaching about secular humanism fit into a discussion about the transcendence and immanence of God and church structure? Just at this point! When the church has no balanced form through which to give a true picture of the nature of God, practical intellectual deism (secular humanism) or superstitious pantheism (New Age, eastern mysticism, the occult) will result.

Structures and forms that reflect half truths about the nature of God have provided fertile soil for the growth of secular humanism and all other kinds of distorted teachings.

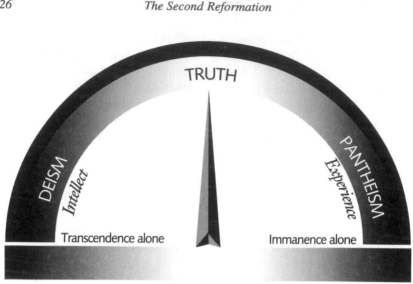

Figure 3. Truth Meter

WHO SHOULD WE BLAME?

Why this "suffocation of the Spirit?" Why does the church go back and forth between the intellect and experience? And why do so many raised in the church jump ship?

The basic error of the church today begins at the point of the nature of God. Who is God and how does He relate to His creation? Is He a watchmaker God who set the scientific laws into motion and then went away? Is He a God living in some spiritual "nether, nether" world, Who is shut out from the real physical world in which man lives? It has been popular to blame the erratic shifts from intellectualism to emotionalism on German theologians and philosophers, who destroy the faith of church members with liberal teachings.

We must also blame ourselves for our spiritual vacuum. We can lean on a predisposition toward academia or a tendency to minister *for* God without relationship *with* God. This inevitably results in our depersonalization of God. We can become spiritually dry even with orthodox theology, a love of God's Word, faithfulness to the church and a personal devotional life.

The problem is not bad theology or insincerity. The problem is the system. When we go through a "summer from hell," we need the immanent presence of God in all of His caring and personal comfort. That kind of relationship is built and maintained over the years in community life with God and fellow believers. When our nightmares come, God must be personally alive in us individually and in community.

JESUS' SIMPLE DESIGN IS ESSENTIAL

Jesus, knowing the heart of man, designed His church in a way to overcome man's temptation to either intellectualize Christianity into a humanistic philosophy (deism) or to experientially distort Christianity into a superstition (pantheism).

The evangelical stream of the church seems to face more danger from biblical intellectualism, resulting in dry orthodoxy. The charismatic stream of the church is more at risk at the point of experience, where emotionalism becomes more important than biblical revelation. It may appear simplistic, but I believe the solution is the same for both the evangelical and charismatic streams which is the return of Jesus' New Testament design of the church in both large group and small group relationships. The church must begin to once again live out the New Testament message in the New Testament method of both large groups and cell groups.

The church can't experience God, as in the first century, without the basic structure of the New Testament church. Part of the suffocation of the Spirit comes because the church has abandoned the small group community design of the church through which Jesus promised to be with us. From personal experience, I believe the cure for academic dryness in our souls is to meet Christ with two or three Christian brothers and sisters as the church, His body. Likewise, the answer for detached emotionalism that misuses and abuses spiritual gifts is the same—accountability in a small group.

We need the New Testament design of the church, meeting together as the "whole church" and as the "home church." We need both, not because of some limitation on God's part, but because of our own limitation when experiencing God. The small group setting keeps reminding us of the nearness of God, of His care, of His intimate comfort. It provides warm and caring community where Christ is in our midst and we are bonded together in our mutual pains and joys.

In heaven, human limitation will not hinder how we experience God. There, we will not be hindered by our inability to relate to a mass of people or to relate to God in His transcendence. "I will know Him even as I am known." But until that time, we are dependent upon three ways of relating to God:

- I meet God as an *individual;*
- I meet God in *mass* with a large number of people;
- I meet God in *community* with a small number of people.

THE DISTORTED PICTURE OF THE CHURCH

The diagram in Figure 4 expresses God's transcendent and immanent manifestation of Himself to His church in its large and small group context. Notice: God provided a way for man to experience Him in His

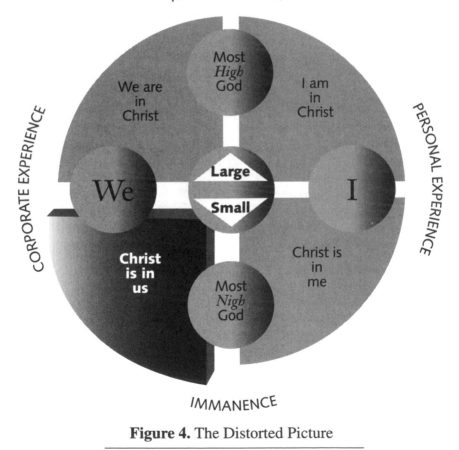

Figure 4. The Distorted Picture

transcendence and immanence in both a personal and corporate context. Christ is in me. That is my personal experience with the immanent God. I am in Christ. That is my personal experience with the transcendent God. We are with Christ. That is our large group corporate experience with the transcendent God. Christ is "in/with us." That is our small group corporate experience with the immanent God.

Take out the lower left quadrant of this diagram, and you have the picture of the incomplete church for the last 1700 years. Except for rare historical periods, the one-winged church has had no way to experience and express God in His immanent closeness in a small group dimension. This has seriously distorted our relationship with God as individuals and the way the world perceives God.

WHY ARE THEY LEAVING THE CHURCH?

According to a new study, "The 'lost generation' of baby boomers, who left mainline Protestantism in the 1970s and '80s is not coming back, and their churches will exert even less of a hold on their children."

Our own members and their children who at one time sat in the pews of our churches have left the church in alarming numbers. Why have they left us?

While they may have left us, many did not leave God! They left our impersonal church structures that were inadequate to put them in touch with a real God involved in real life. Our one-winged church structure gave them an incomplete picture of God, a picture of a God far away and unapproachable. It gave them an institutional God of rules and legalism, not of love; a God of buildings and committees, not relationships; a God of information transmission, not a God of experiential transformation; a God of behavioral modification, not of spiritual sanctification. It gave them a God of emotionalism, not of spiritual power.

Why did they leave? Benton Johnson, a University of Oregon sociology professor, suggested: "It's just that the church doesn't do anything for them."[5] In what way is the church failing them? It would seem the complaint is not at the point of information. The one-winged church has disseminated information about God to them. Neither has the church failed to entertain. The church in the past two decades has been marketed for its greatest entertainment appeal. However, the church has been unable to make God vital to them down in real life.

Man can't tolerate God's absence from the world for a long time. If the church doesn't live in His indwelling presence as the "most nigh" God, then the world will intellectually design its own watchmaker god, will experientially revert to pantheism, or will drop out. The world is too frightening without God and does not make sense without the presence of the spiritual within the physical world. Therefore, man will take the leap of faith from reason (intellectual deism) to experience and feeling (spiritual pantheism).

The end result is that a large portion of the church, while knowing about God, has not experienced the power of God in personal living. Relationship with God was sacrificed at the altar of knowledge about God. Consequently, community was sacrificed to individual experience. The church's one-winged large group informational culture gives little meaning or hope in what Francis Schaeffer called "the tough stuff of life."

> "There is no use saying you have community or love for each other if it does not get down into the tough stuff of life. . . . I am convinced that in the 20th century people all over the world will not listen if we have the right doctrine, the right polity, but are not exhibiting community."[6]

We find ourselves along with Professor Wallace expressing a cognitive belief system: "I believe that . . ." instead of living in a personal relationship that says "I trust in . . . ."

BAND-AIDS WON'T WORK

Some churches, after researching what the contemporary generation wants, are trying to give them the experience they demand. The strategy is to package the church in a new way so that members get more experience and less knowledge. However, without a New Testament small group of transparent fellowship, the church will be no more successful on the experience side than it was on the knowledge side.

In their book *What's Gone Wrong with the Harvest?*, Engel and Norton conclude, "The answer does not lie in renewal of old forms, because that often is an attempt only to place band-aids on the exterior wounds of the old shell."[7]

Band-aids on the outside won't do! The problem is the system itself. No matter how many times the church responds to the perceived needs of its members for either knowledge or experience, the problem will not be solved. The solution to the problem doesn't lie in the perceived needs of the members or unbelievers. Jesus has already solved the problem of man's flip-flopping back and forth between knowledge and experience. The solution is for the church to be the body of Christ through which He lives and reveals Himself in transcendent greatness and immanent comfort.

PART III

JESUS' REVOLUTIONARY DESIGN FOR THE CHURCH

*There is a new style of church life that is so biblical
it predates the [modern] church as we know it,
but so "future" it can't be put into "old wineskins."*
—Ralph Neighbour

13

JESUS' BASIC BUILDING BLOCK

If God, as we believe, is truly revealed in the life of
Christ, the most important thing to Him is the
creation of centers of loving fellowship, which in
turn infect the world.
—Elton Trueblood

Every important event in Christ's life took place in some form of community. More often than not, it was in a small group context. Jesus came down from heaven out of the trinitarian community of the Father, Son and Spirit—the original two or three gathered together. He was born and grew to manhood in the Jewish family, a community of Joseph and Mary. He was baptized at the river in the midst of John's community of followers. For three and a half years, He lived with twelve leaders who were His special community. The transfiguration was experienced in community as Peter, James and John went with Him to the mountain, where His countenance was changed.

As the cross loomed larger, the experiences he had in community became even more important to Him. In the Upper Room, Jesus washed the feet of the disciples. He taught them, modeled servanthood, and walked them through His death and resurrection, all within a community setting. He led them out to the Garden of Gethsemane for the last moment of prayer as a community.

He was crucified with the community of thieves on the cross, being numbered with the transgressors. Though in disarray, distressed and diminished in number, the community waited at the foot of the cross. The women remained with Him until the terrible end as a grieving community, yet doing what was necessary to give comfort and prepare His body for burial.

This tiny fellowship clung together as a frightened community during those dark hours when Jesus was in the tomb. Broken? Yes! Fearful? Yes; but still together in *community*. To a frightened community, the women brought news about the risen Christ.

The resurrection appearances for the most part took place in a community context. The two disciples on the road to Emmaus recognized Him as the One who had broken bread with them at the table in community. At the first appearance in the Upper Room, Jesus revealed Himself to the community as more than a spirit. One week later, again in the Upper Room, He appeared to the community of faith and breathed His Spirit upon them. These appearances were all in the settings where their hearts had joined His in community.

He appeared to them as a group for the third time at the seaside where they were fishing. He prepared breakfast for the disciples and encouraged and taught them that morning *as a community*.

Jesus' ascension party on the Mount consisted of a large community numbering upwards of 500 (1 Corinthians 15:6). Ten days later, while together and of one accord, the promised Spirit fell upon that community in the upper room. No wonder the early Christians "devoted themselves . . . to the fellowship" after His ascension (Acts 2:42). *Community* was their context for living with Christ for more than three years.

MARY AND MARTHA GROUPS

Jesus established the church as community during the first century—built around a personal relationship with Himself. In Luke 10:38-42, Jesus gave an example of the focus of this community in the story of Mary and Martha:

> Now as they were traveling along, he entered a certain village; and a woman named Martha welcomed him into her home. And she had a sister called Mary, who moreover was listening to the Lord's word, seated at his feet. But Martha was distracted with all her preparations; and she came up to Him, and said, "Lord, do You not care that my sister has left me to do all the serving alone? Then tell her to help me." But the Lord answered and said to her,

"Martha, Martha, you are worried and bothered about so many things; but only a few things are necessary, really only one, for Mary has chosen the good part, which shall not be taken away from her."

The actions of these sisters represent two ways of approaching Christ:

The Martha Approach: *Performance for Christ*

 • Perform a service for Christ
 • Expect others to help do something for Christ
 • Make something happen for Christ
 • Prepare for Christ's presence or coming
 • Run everything smoothly for Christ
 • Coordinate Christ's schedule
 • Get busy for the Lord to the point of distraction
 • Visit with Christ in passing as you do your work
 • Complain to Christ about the service of others
 • Fulfill your duty even if relationships suffer
 • Focus most of all on what is secondary

The Mary Approach: *Person of Christ*

 • Enter into Christ's presence
 • Sit at Christ's feet
 • Look into Christ's face
 • Listen to Christ's voice
 • Receive Christ's power
 • Expect Christ's healing from all hurts
 • Feel Christ's gentle touch
 • Know Christ's unconditional acceptance
 • Rest in Christ's love
 • Be a child in Christ's arms
 • Experience Christ's freedom
 • Release all fear to Christ
 • Wash Christ's feet (John 12:1-8)
 • Do Christ's will from an overflow of His presence
 • Focus first of all on what is better

CHORES—OR CHRIST?

Martha may be the most defended person in the Bible: don't say anything bad about Martha or you will be rebuffed with comments like, "She is serving;" "If everyone just sat around meditating, nothing would ever get done;" "Someone has to do it!"

In many sermons from this passage, Martha is elevated to sainthood. "Martha hands and a Mary heart" makes a good sermon title, even if it has little to do with the truth of this passage. Jesus is not praising Martha's hands, or ours. He is praising Mary's heart to enter His presence and turn loose of the need to please Him by the work of her hands. Mary understood the importance of community.

The story about Mary and Martha is not about who does the dishes, sweeps the floor, and prepares the meal. Jesus' concern and displeasure with Martha is at the point of her relationship and attitude toward Him. Martha is so busy doing for Him she has no time to be with Him.

Can you see Martha waving at Jesus as she hurried about doing her chores? She might say, "It's wonderful to have you with us, Lord. I don't have time to visit with you, because I am so busy making everything right for your visit. Please make Mary get up and help also!"

This is characteristic of the *doer* for Christ. Everyone else must *do* what they are doing. Not only does Martha see her own significance before Christ in what she does, but she judges everyone else in the same way. In Martha's mind, Mary was wrong for not helping her prepare the meal for Christ. Jesus corrected her explaining the importance of *being* over *doing*. With Jesus, being always preceded doing.

Jesus said Mary focused on what is better and Martha on what is secondary. Our relationship with Christ must be priority. Nothing must hinder that. No work we do, even spiritual work, can substitute for our relationship with Christ, being with Him, focusing our lives and time upon Him.

If Martha had entered into Jesus' presence, all of the chores would have been completed in due time and probably with a lot more joy. Jesus and Mary would have done whatever was necessary to help. If Martha had been honest, she would have admitted she really was not doing all of that work for Jesus. She was doing it to satisfy her own need for significance. The most faithful "Marthas" are those who believe their significance and salvation depends upon what they do for Jesus.

ARE WE "BEING HIS WORKMANSHIP" OR WORKING FOR JESUS?

"For we are His workmanship, created in Christ Jesus for good works, which God prepared beforehand, that we should walk in them" (Ephesians 2:10). Being His workmanship and working for Christ are two entirely different approaches to the Christian life. As the cell group focuses on Christ, we come to understand the difference. In His presence, we become His workmanship through His power working in us, and then we walk in good works. Evidently Mary knew the difference between being His workmanship and working for Him. She wanted to be with Him first of all. Poor Martha didn't seem to have a clue about this truth.

Many of the present small groups found in church life are Martha groups which are performance driven, task oriented, work consumed, activity centered and duty bound. Jesus is no more pleased with performance-centered small groups today than He was with Martha's relationship based on performance in the first century. Jesus did not teach us to be "Marthas" who join together in a work contract to do something for Him. Jesus joins us together in Mary-type groups to sit together at His feet and to be prepared to be His workmanship.

Why are our groups usually Martha groups focusing on performance? Our *corporate* way of approaching Christ grows out of our *personal* way of approaching Christ. The groups we participate in reflect our individual relationship to Christ. Many of us are Martha-type Christians ourselves, focusing on performance in our individual lives. When we come together in groups, we focus on tasks and activities because that is the way we approach God personally. Studying about Christ or doing something for Him is more comfortable than having intimate close relationships with Him in a group setting. That's why we defend Martha to the death. Never doubt it: death is the end of performance for Christ. Performance for Christ will ultimately kill freedom, grace and joy in serving Christ personally or in a group.

AN EXAMPLE OF A MARY CELL

The attitude of the heart is the key to a Mary cell, but the heart does express itself in practical patterns. Whatever pattern we use for cell life should be built around encounter with Christ. One such pattern I call the three P's: Christ's Presence, Christ's Power, and Christ's Purpose. The following is not the only pattern for experiencing Christ. It does, however, provide a picture for what I am talking about when I refer to a Mary cell. Take this agenda and use it to experience His Presence and see the difference between a Mary cell and Martha cell. It can provide a starting place for you as your church develops your own cell meeting pattern.

SAMPLE CELL AGENDA

Ice Breaker: What was the best thing that happened to you this past week and why?

Acknowledge Christ's Presence:

Leader states: We are here to experience Christ. Christ said, "Where two or three are gathered together in my name there I am in their midst." He also said, "I will not leave you orphans, I will come to you." We believe Jesus does what He promised. Therefore, we acknowledge His presence and welcome Him into our midst.

Have a time of prayer to thank Jesus for His presence in the group.

Sing some songs of praise and worship. (If you have a guitar player, this is helpful. But the meeting is not dependent on the musical talent in the group.) Remember: Christ is in the midst of your group leading you in worship to the Father.

Experience Christ's Power:

Read Luke 10:38-42. Pick from the following questions those which you sense the Holy Spirit leading you to discuss:

1. How did Martha get her significance?
2. How did Mary get her significance?
3. Do you most often identify with Martha or Mary? Why?
4. Did Martha feel the occasion was a "success" or somehow less than it ought to be? Why did she feel that way?
5. How did Mary feel about the occasion? Why did she feel so?

6. What is the "better thing" in this passage?
7. What are the "many things" that distract, worry, and upset you to the point that you cannot focus on the "better thing?" If you focused on the "better thing," would the "many things" still get done?" (Read Matt. 6:33.)
8. What needs to happen in your life so you can have a Mary attitude toward Christ?

Ask: What work of His power does Christ wish to do in my life right now?

Do not be afraid of silence at this time. If no one feels led to share after five minutes of silence, then proceed immediately to the next part. Often someone will share a need that Christ wishes to address in their lives which will provide opportunity for prayer, ministry and edification.

Fulfill Christ's Purpose:

Ask: How does Christ want to use me to touch the hurts in the world?

Give opportunity to each person to share: This week Christ wants to use me to . . . pray for John, bake a cake for the new single guy who moved in down the street, witness to my neighbor, etc.

Close with prayer for the specific ministry visions God has given.

OUR ONLY AGENDA, JESUS

What is the agenda of cell groups? He is! Jesus, Himself, is the agenda. He is the one essential factor in the life of His called-out community on earth. You may have tried focusing on worship, ministry, therapy, discipleship, Bible Study, or evangelism in an effort to duplicate the dynamic of New Testament small group life. These approaches might work for one meeting or for a short time, but they will not sustain the dynamic growth and power of the New Testament church over a long period. Burnout is sure to come when the focus is on anything other than Christ.

In fact, all of the above agendas for a cell group can better take place in another setting. Worship in a larger setting might be more moving. Ministry might be better in a group focused expressly on deliverance. Therapy can be more effective in a group led by trained counselors. Fellowship may be better down at the pub or some other social event. Bible Study Fellowship and other such groups may do a better job of teaching the Bible. Social action groups can do a better job of exerting pressure that brings about political change. Para-church groups who devote themselves solely to discipleship or evangelism may appear more fruitful in their specialized areas than a cell group.

Christ in the midst of His people is the one dynamic that can't be duplicated in any other type of group. This is unique. No other group expects this, prepares for it, or claims it. Only groups that live in the presence, power and purpose of Christ as their intentional focus will experience the incarnate, indwelling, resurrected and living presence of Christ in their midst. These are *Christ-groups* just as surely as I am a *Christ-ian.*

Will we give up the uniqueness of Christ as our central focus for all of the other spiritual agendas? No! Christ is the dynamic of the cell and the format we use should allow Christ to operate the cell and live in it. When Jesus becomes the agenda, all the other agendas are realized. All other spiritual agendas are by-products of Him. As Robert Raines encouraged:

> The *koinonia* groups provide the context in which the institutional church may begin to become the Body of Christ, and in which nominal church members may become disciples of Christ. Within such groups Christians are being equipped for the work of ministry, first in the church and then in the world.[1]

14

JESUS' REVOLUTIONARY SYSTEM

The system is the solution.
—AT&T

M any organizations, including some churches, argue that they would have few problems if the workers did their jobs correctly. This may be a logical conclusion, but is it correct? Is the problem with the organization, with the workers, or with the system?

Dr. Joseph M. Juran is among the quality control experts who maintain that changing the systems through which work is done has the potential to eliminate mistakes and errors. Dr. Juran says, "This is the 85/15 rule: At least 85% of organizational problems can be corrected by changing systems (which are largely determined by management) and less than 15% are under a worker's control . . ."[1]

Dr. Juran would diagnose the problem of the church to be systems breakdown, not a personnel weakness. However, we make the general conclusion that the people are the weak link of the church. Thus, we have tried to improve the quality of the people, motivate them, even make them feel guilty so they will give better effort. We educate them, preach at them, train them, all to no avail.

Lyle Schaller, in his book *The Change Agent,* recognizes the helplessness of sincere people trying to bring change within a faulty system.

"Unless there is a change in the direction, value system, and orientation of the organization, frequently there are severe limitations on what can be accomplished by changes in people or by the addition of new personnel."[2]

Michael Gerber, author of *The E-Myth*, suggests an important question every organization should ask: "How can I create a business whose results are systems dependent rather than people dependent?" He is not saying people are not important. "People bring systems to life. People make it possible for things that are designed to work to produce the intended results."[3] He adds, "The system runs the business. The people run the system."[4] From a Christian perspective we might add, "God runs the people."

According to Gerber, "But for ordinary people to do extraordinary things a system—a 'way of doing things'—is needed to compensate for the disparity between the skills your people have and the skills needed to produce the result. . . . you will be forced to find a system that leverages your ordinary people to the point where they can produce extraordinary results."[5]

When church leaders accept the fact that the church system creates the majority of problems, they will understand the futility in trying to change themselves or their members until the system is changed.

A Church System

How do we define a *system?* Gerber says: "A system is a set of things, actions, ideas, and information that interact with each other, and in so doing alter other systems."[6]

Using the concept of a system to understand the church isn't necessarily an unspiritual, secular exercise. God is the creator of systems. The universe itself is a system; so we use the term solar system. A system approach to the church simply recognizes the church is made up of different parts which fit together in an integrated form by design. Paul uses the word administration or plan in Ephesians to explain the working system of the church.

> He made known to us the mystery of His will, according to His kind intention which He purposed in Him with a view to an administration suitable to the fullness of the times, that is, the summing up of all things in Christ, things in the heavens and things upon the earth (Ephesians 1:9-10).

And to bring to light what is the administration of the mystery which for ages has been hidden in God, who created all things, in order that the manifold wisdom of God might now be made known through the church to the rulers and the authorities in the heavenly places (Ephesians 3:9-10).

Among the most frequently used metaphors in the New Testament to describe the church are "body," "family" and "building." These metaphors in one way or another are integrated and interrelated systems. The body is an organic living system. A family is the most basic social system. A building is a structural system.

Paul seems to prefer the concept of body as a metaphor for the church and uses it in 1 Corinthians. 12:12-27. In Ephesians and Colossians, this theme is further developed. Christ is the head of the church which is his body (Ephesians 1:22, 5:23, Colossians 1:18, 24). The body metaphor portrays the church as a living organism rather than as an organization, an incarnation system through which God indwells His church.

James F. Hind, author of the *Heart and Soul of Effective Management: A Christian approach to Managing and Motivating People* shares a keen insight into Jesus' management style. Hind suggests Jesus operated as a manager which implies some kind of a systems context.

In only three years he defined a mission and formed strategies to carry it out. With a staff of 12 unlikely men, he organized Christianity, which today has branches in all the world's countries and a 32.4 percent share of the world's population, twice as big as its nearest rival. Managers want to develop people to their full potential, taking ordinary people and making them extraordinary. This is what Christ did with his disciples. Jesus was the most effective executive in history. The results he achieved are second to none.[7]

Jesus was the divine implementor of the divine system. The church is an extension of the system Jesus carefully built during the last three and a half years of His life on earth. Examining the system's essential elements should be the beginning point for implementing Jesus' divine system today.

LOOKING FOR A SYSTEM

I began my quest for a church system while serving as a missionary in Thailand. My search was driven by two observations:

- Radical methods were necessary to reach a Buddhist country.
- Current systems would not result in a New Testament church model.

Everywhere I looked I saw a need for radical change! To understand the nature of change, I looked for books on this subject. Lyle Schaller, in *The Change Agent,* included a five step process of change. The process, detailed below, has become invaluable to me in understanding how church systems change.

1. **Convergence of interest caused by discontent with the status quo.** A new idea breaks in upon the status quo and causes confrontation. The convergence of the old and the new is always part of a change process. Schaller says "in any discussion of intentional change it is almost impossible to overstate the importance of discontent. Without discontent with the present situation there can be no . . . change."[8] If the new idea remains only a new idea fed by discontent, change will never take place.

2. **Establishment of an initiating strategy group.** Someone must take the initiative and believe in the new idea enough to act upon it. A catalytic visionary or two believe the new idea and begin to promote it. However, if two or three initiators are convinced of the idea yet can't convince anyone else, the new idea will never catch on. Other initiators must come on board.

3. **Legitimating and sponsorship of the idea through the development of a core group.** A broader group must own the idea along with the visionaries. The idea must have other sponsors who will legitimize the concept. However, the idea will still not take off until it is actually implemented.

4. **Mobilization and implementation of resources.** The idea is implemented and put into motion. Only if the vision becomes a viable model will the change actually take place. Advocating change and implementing change are two entirely different matters. It is not enough to conceptually embrace a new idea; it must also be established as a proven way to operate. Forms and tracks must be laid by which the vision can actually be put into action.

5. **Fulfillment of charter by freezing at the new level of performance.** After the idea is set into motion and the change is actually implemented, the idea must be frozen so those continuing to implement the new idea will not slip back into the old way of operating.[9]

When I first read this analysis of the change process, I knew it applied to what God had called me to do in developing a system for building the church. However, I had no frame of reference upon which to hang the change concepts. For more than five years, I filed away these ideas about the change process while continuing my search, primarily in Acts and the Epistles, for a workable (and New Testament) church system.

15

JESUS' CONTINUUM

Every activity, every job is part of a process.
A flow diagram of any process will
divide the work into stages.
—W. Edwards Deming

A fter searching Acts and the Epistles for a New Testament church pattern, I turned to the Gospels for some help. I hoped to find the essential nature and design of the church in Jesus' ministry. After all, the first century church in Acts and the Epistles developed out of the model Jesus gave His followers. This search was driven by several questions. Did Jesus have a process in mind when he began the first church? Was there a pattern or plan?

FRUSTRATING SEARCH

My search in the Gospels for a church planting process began in frustration and disappointment. The Gospel events seemed random and disconnected. I examined a harmony of the gospels, but I could find no harmony in the development of the Church.

I knew the four books were written from different perspectives in order to give a broader picture of who Jesus was and what He was doing. Matthew was one of the twelve disciples called while a despised tax collector. One suspects he may have been older than some of the other disciples because of his government position. Mark saw the events first hand as a young lad growing up in a home which was perhaps the location of many early church meetings. He was undoubtedly influenced by the first-hand accounts of Peter and Barnabas. On the other hand, Luke wrote as an educated historian and carefully used eyewitnesses for the basis of his book. John, one of Jesus' inner circle, gave a spiritual history of the life of Jesus to supplement the historical record. With these four pictures of the life of Christ, I continued to search the Gospels for Jesus' systematic pattern for building the Church.

NUMBERS ARE MARKERS

The breakthrough came when I noticed the numbers of people Jesus worked with at each stage. Different numbers consistently show up in each of the Gospel accounts. These numbers were significant in how Jesus built His church:

• Two who were *Innovators;*
• Three who composed an *Inner Circle;*
• Twelve who He gathered as *Core Leaders;*
• 70 who comprised His *Support Network;*
• 120 who became the first *Base Congregation;*
• 3000 and 5000 who were *Converts.*

Jesus followed a continuum during His three and a half year ministry, and the numbers help identify the process. Webster's dictionary defines a continuum as: "a continuous quantity, series, or whole."[1] A continuum is a continuous action. Only from outside the continuum can one distinguish between its parts and see what is happening.

Shortly after discovering these groups, a light turned on for me. I remembered the change process discussed in Schaller's book. Jesus' approach to change in the first century predated by almost 2,000 years the process of change cited by Schaller. Jesus' church planting continuum followed a universal change process. In the first century, Jesus operated out of an *incremental leadership strategy.* Each stage was built upon previous ones.

JESUS' DIVINE GOSPEL SYSTEM

The Gospels provide a frame of reference for understanding what the church is, how it operates and how it is begun. This doesn't play Paul against Jesus. Jesus modeled the first church design, and then Paul and other first century leaders instinctively followed it.

We can better understand and appreciate the more advanced Church of the Epistles after seeing what Jesus did in the Gospels. Jesus built His church in the Epistles in the same way He built the first church in the Gospels.

During my study of the Gospels, I related Schaller's change model to the church stages in the Gospel continuum. Figure 5 shows how the continuum relates to Jesus' numbers (column 3) and Schaller's change model (column 2). This grid will serve as a guide for our discussion through the remainder of the book. The remaining pages of this chapter are an overview of Jesus' continuum (column 4).

Strategic Phases	Schaller's Change Process	New Testament Numbers	Jesus' Continuum	Vision Action
Preparation	Convergence	Prophetic Word (Jesus)	Cell Church Vision	Conceived
PROTOTYPE	Initiating Set	2-3 people	Innovation	Introduced
	Legitimating Sponsorship	12 people	Core Leadership	Owned
	Execution Set	70 people	Support Network	Implemented
Critical Mass / OPERATIONAL	Fulfillment of Charter	120 people	Base Congregation	Empowered
		3000-5000	Church Expansion	Expanded

Figure 5. Continuum Grid

JESUS' CONVERGENCE STAGE

The Convergence Stage is the time of preparation before a new idea is put into action within the status quo. After 400 years of prophetic silence, God broke into history in the lives of Mary and Joseph, and Elizabeth and Zachariah. That prophetic movement can be summed up in the word incarnation, Immanuel, God with us, Jesus. God become part of the universe He created. This act radically impacted the Roman government, Greek philosophy, Judaism, and the pagan world. The transcendent Creator became immanent. The Word had become flesh and that flesh now had a name, a people, a history, a time, and a place. Incarnation had a space on earth at a particular time in history. In the fullness of time God's incarnation converged with history with a dramatic voice and life.

JESUS' INNOVATION STAGE

During the Innovation Stage, the vision is introduced by catalytic leaders. Jesus and John the Baptist were the two catalysts for setting the vision in motion. John's task was temporary—he was like a "voice in the wilderness." Jesus' ministry was anything but a temporary voice. He was establishing a spiritual body (the church) through which He would live until the second coming.

John moved out of the desert with the mission of preparing the way for the Messiah. Jesus then came preaching the Kingdom. John and Jesus met in the waters of the Jordan River where the Father announced Christ as the Incarnate Son "with whom He was well pleased."

Why did Jesus need John? One innovator was not enough. John had to be present in the Innovation Stage to declare who Jesus really was. We see different kinds of innovators or catalysts at work here. There are catalysts who prepares the way (John), who establishes the way (Jesus) and who are prepared to lead in the way (Peter, James and John). The vision had to be put into motion so the idea could take shape and form. This was the initiating strategy group.

When establishing a cell church, there must be two or three who have the vision deeply set within their hearts. They are *prophets,* who see what does not yet exist as though it had already happened. They are prepared to pay any price to make the vision reality. In the case of John, he paid with his head, while Jesus paid with His crucifixion.

JESUS' LEADERSHIP CORE STAGE

The leadership core stage provides a group to own and oversee the vision. Even though Jesus began to preach to the multitudes, He had another agenda in mind. Jesus called out a core group to model His *ecclesia* or "called out ones." This core stage consisted of twelve leaders chosen because of their potential for obedience, not because of their learning or ability.

Jesus poured His life and time into His core leaders. They formed His basic community through which He would prepare future leaders. Jesus was forming a wineskin into which the incarnation wine would be poured. That wineskin was not just for the Day of Pentecost but for every generation until Jesus returned. Robert Raines has helped us apply this to our own situation:

> We must train a hard core of committed and growing disciples who shall serve as leaven within the local church. We have ample biblical authority for the training of such a hard core. This is precisely what Jesus did with the twelve disciples. We read in the eighth, ninth, and tenth chapters of the Gospel according to Mark that Jesus took these closest friends apart from the crowds and taught them the conditions of discipleship. He was deliberately training them for leadership after His death. It wasn't the crowds to whom Jesus preached, but this little group of men that became the foundation of the early church. Paul preached to the crowds in synagogues, on public squares, wherever he could reach them; but it wasn't the crowds, it was the little groups of people in Galatia, in Philippi, in Corinth, with whom Paul lived and worked for several months at a time, which became the foundation of the Mediterranean churches.[2]

JESUS' SUPPORT NETWORK STAGE

The support network stage gathers together those who will implement the vision. Jesus equipped and trained His core group and an extended family network over a period of about three years. The support network grew from the twelve to the seventy, who were often deployed two by two.

In this learning process, the disciples asked Jesus all of the wrong questions; why, when, where, what, and how? Jesus kept answering one question, Who? Jesus would build His church through His presence and power, not their knowledge or ability. This was the primary lesson taught during the support network stage.

Jesus implemented His divine system through His loyal support network. An embryonic community was formed by Jesus consisting of the seventy. No stage in Jesus' continuum is more important than this one. In your own ministry, this stage will take place as the leadership core begins to draw in family members and other close friends who become committed to the vision.

JESUS' BASE CONGREGATION STAGE

The base congregation forms the unit where power for ministry and multiplication can happen. In the upper room, 120 disciples waited in obedience to the Lord. Jesus' promise recorded in John 14 came true. In the experience of Pentecost, Jesus came to them; Jesus and the Father abided with them; the Spirit was in them and with them. Everything was now in place for exponential multiplication to take place through that congregation, and it did! The base congregation was empowered for the vision.

JESUS' CHURCH STAGE

The incarnated Christ in His new spiritual body—the church, coordinated the multiplication of cells, congregations and churches in "Jerusalem, Judea, Samaria, and the ends of the earth." Many were added to the church, 3000 the first time and 5000 soon after. The church expanded the vision.

If a 120 member church today has fifty new converts, it has great difficulty conserving and integrating them into the body. How did the church after Pentecost integrate 3,000 and then 5,000 more? We must realistically understand the church at this time numbered more than just the 120 core disciples mentioned in the Upper Room. We know that ten days before Pentecost, 500 had assembled for Jesus' ascension. However, even with a 500 member church the ability to absorb 8,000 new members in a short period of time is astounding. How was this done?

Jesus had modeled for more than three years the structure through which large numbers could be integrated into the church. Just like a family unit, the cell of twelve, with an inner circle of Peter, James and John, could absorb large numbers and effectively care for them. This is why they went from house to house, daily. This was the context through which this number of new believers could be cared for, taught and absorbed into the original group of believers. Daily pointed to the time necessary to integrate thousands of new believers into the body of Christ. The small groups meeting in homes gave the first century church a way to absorb and nurture growth that was four or five times larger than their core congregation.

In addition to the home meetings, large group gatherings provided a way for the Apostles to bring them together in special events. The world could now see their unity, the gospel could be reviewed and shared, and the vision of reaching the world could be cast.

Note: Each stage of Jesus' continuum will be discussed in detail in the following pages. Figure 5 on page 151 will help you understand how the different elements fit together. This continuum grid will be placed at the beginning of each stage with the elements of the grid that are related to that stage highlighted. Chapters 16 and 17 describe the prototype phase of beginning or transitioning into a cell church. Chapters 18-22 walk through the units of Jesus' continuum in more detail and provide practical insights on how to implement the strategy. This process will lead you to critical mass, the launching pad for the operational cell church which is discussed in chapters 21 and 22.

Strategic Phases	Schaller's Change Process	New Testament Numbers	Jesus' Continuum	Vision Action
Preparation	Convergence	Prophetic Word (Jesus)	Cell Church Vision	Conceived
PROTOTYPE	Initiating Set	2-3 people	Innovation	Introduced
	Legitimating Sponsorship	12 people	Core Leadership	Owned
	Execution Set	70 people	Support Network	Implemented
Critical Mass / OPERATIONAL	Fulfillment of Charter	120 people	Base Congregation	Empowered
		3000-5000	Church Expansion	Expanded

16
JESUS' PROTOTYPE

*The Prototype becomes the working model of the
dream; it is the dream in microcosm.*
—Michael E. Gerber

A couple of years ago, a pastor flew into Houston to talk about cell churches. He was highly motivated and challenged by the cell church vision after reading *Where Do We Go From Here?* When I picked him up at the airport, I quickly sensed his frustration, and even a little anger. His expectations for beginning a cell church were not being realized and he couldn't put all the pieces together. He was suffering from a common cell church disease I would later identify as ICC Syndrome: *Instant Cell Church Syndrome.* W. Edwards Deming describes this sickness as "instant pudding:"

> Companies chase fads and look for a quick fix to complex problems if they have no constancy of purpose. The quick fix provides only temporary comfort and makes it appear as if something is happening. It is, according to Deming, only "instant pudding" and not the kind of program that is well conceived and developed through a focus on the future.[1]

INSTANT CELL CHURCH SYNDROME

This malady is fatal to a cell church vision if not diagnosed and treated in time.

Symptoms of ICC Syndrome include:
1. Expecting multiplication during the preparation stages
2. Changing structures without first changing values
3. Depending on methods and materials rather than on principles and concepts
4. Attaching cell groups as an appendage to the existing one-winged structure
5. Servicing a high maintenance Sunday service while trying to establish a cell base

ICC Syndrome is transmitted:
1. When reading books about the cell church movement which challenge and cast a vision about cell churches without adequately explaining the process or time frame for becoming that kind of church
2. By visionaries who excite leaders about post-pentecost type results without preparing them to pay the pre-pentecost price necessary to establish an Operational model
3. From pilgrimages to large Operational cell churches where the finished product is showcased without adequately explaining the developmental years
4. At seminars and conferences where Operational strategies are suggested without taking into account the three and a half year preparation process of Jesus Christ

Most of all, ICC syndrome is a disease of our own heart. Like Esau we sell our future birthright for a quick bowl of porridge in order to satisfy immediate gratification.

Instant Cell Church Syndrome is highly contagious and primarily spread by existing cell churches suffering from Prototype amnesia when they forget what it was like at the beginning of the transition into cells. The person who believes he can make a few minor adjustments to the existing church and become an Operational cell church is already ICC Positive.

THE CURE

The cure for ICC Syndrome is to develop a Prototype. Michael Gerber explains this term for us:

> To the franchiser, the Prototype becomes the working model of the dream; it is the dream in microcosm. The Prototype becomes the incubator and the nursery for all creative thought, the station where creativity is nursed by pragmatism to grow into an innovation that works.
>
> The franchise Prototype is also the place where all assumptions are put to the test to see how well they work before becoming operational in the business. . . . The Prototype acts as a buffer between hypothesis and action.[2]

A good dose of learning more about Jesus' ministry when He designed the first cell church will cure ICC Syndrome. Jesus' ministry on earth was the prototype period for the first church. Allowing Jesus to walk us through His three and a half year prototype will do wonders for those stricken with this disease. The cure has the best chance of being successful upstream at the beginning of the process, not downstream at the operational stage when the disease has already become full blown. The recovery period is from three to five years in most cases.

Jesus prepared His salvation, His system, and His servants to receive and operate in His Spirit during His three and a half years of ministry. Jesus walked the disciples step by step through the growth continuum necessary to build the foundation for exponential growth at Pentecost. The Prototype period is the time when:

1. Vision is discovered and cast.
2. Values are defined and internalized.
3. Leadership is identified and developed.
4. Body life is experienced and modeled.
5. Infrastructure is tested and experienced.
6. Power is anticipated and received.

Those who have been given a cell church vision by God must first of all develop a prototype before the vision can become operational.

GET IT RIGHT IN THE BEGINNING

Jesus meticulously followed the growth continuum to build the first church model. He began with two or three innovators, then grew to 12 leaders, added up to 70 in a support network, which became 120 in the upper room. Certain lessons had to be learned and certain stages passed through before the congregational base would be formed and the church could experience rapid multiplication. These stages during the prototype phase are essential to the eventual multiplication of the church.

The stages can be accelerated but not completely bypassed. During the prototype phase each stage prepares the congregation to live together in cell community and move toward multiplication. If any stage is bypassed, the church will have to compensate or go back and learn the lesson skipped. This will add time to the prototype stage because corrections and adjustments must be made.

Quality control experts such as W. Edwards Deming and J. M. Juran teach the importance of getting it right in the beginning. The prototype phase is all about quality control at the point of the initial design. If it isn't done right in the beginning, it must be corrected later on. According to their calculations, it is 50 times more difficult to fix a problem after the process has been done wrong than to do the job right in the first place.

My father was a contractor and a bricklayer. Many times my brother and I went with him to lay out a job. We would fetch tools, hold the tape as he measured, and spot the surveying stick so he could lay out the floor plan. We would then drive in stakes, nail batter boards in place and help him stretch lines that would serve as the outline of the building. Before the crew arrived on the scene, my father knew he had to set the prototype which was the guide for what the building would eventually become. If the building was not begun properly the consequences were expensive and time consuming. To go back and correct work done in the wrong way was very difficult, especially if the wall was a brick one. My father had never heard of the quality control theory that a job is 50 times harder to repair, but from practical experience, he operated out of it.

Get it right at the Prototype phase, and the model is easier to implement during the Operational phase. Get it wrong in the beginning, and you will add headaches, heartaches, frustration and time to the overall process.

To my knowledge, every existing large cell church processed through some kind of Prototype phase, either by design or providence. Cell churches simply do not arrive on the scene full blown.

PROTOTYPE AMNESIA

During the past two decades, church leaders from all over the world have made pilgrimages to operational cell churches in different parts of the world. Invariably, they drew all the wrong conclusions about how those large cell churches relate to their church situation. They tried to implement operational cell church methods rather than use cell church prototype methods.

Why do sincere leaders have problems reproducing what they see while visiting large cell churches? It is because these large operational cell churches typically explain what is presently happening in their churches, not what happened ten or more years ago as their growth was set into motion. Large cell churches suffer from a form of amnesia about their prototype stage.

A leader of a traditional church cannot expect the structure of a large operational cell church (for instance the Yoido Full Gospel Church in Seoul) to be appropriate for his situation. The principles and concepts may be the same, but the stages of development are light years apart. It is necessary to discover what happened 30 years ago at that massive church. The operating strategy of a 750,000 member church is not what is needed. Instead, the church leader should examine the original transition strategy.

This model is replicated by developing the visionary leadership, the support network, its commitment to cells, the simple organization, its base congregation remnant, and the theology of New Testament cells. These were the ingredients used to change this traditional church into the largest cell church in the world. Operational cell churches should spend as much time teaching other churches about their prototype pilgrimage as they do their current operational procedures.

THE FATAL ASSUMPTION

It is fatal to assume that just because we understand the mechanics of the cell church, we understand the cell church. The cell church is much more than the mechanics. Without the dynamics, principles, philosophy of life behind it, the mechanics are lifeless forms. The only way we can understand cell church life is to experience it.

Just as Jesus walked through those three and a half years with His first church, through the Spirit, He walks through the three and a half year preparation period with every church willing to follow. As Jesus gave His personal attention to building the first church, He gives His personal attention to building the church today.

If we are going to be the unique kind of church we see in the pages of the New Testament, we must follow Jesus in a time of preparation and relearning. That relearning and preparation is especially necessary for leaders, the very ones who most often impatiently look for shortcuts and ways to become an instant cell church. In light of all we need to learn about being Christ's kind of church, we should be grateful we have the prototype phase to get it right.

Let us not forget that Jesus, while in the flesh, was giving intensive direction to just one church start, and it still took three and a half years. This is the question: would the church have exploded after the Spirit came, if Jesus had not already carefully prepared a base congregation, a leadership structure, and a cell community infrastructure? I do not believe so!

The problem lies not with the Spirit, but with our yielding to life in the Spirit. I must be prepared to be part of the kind of church that depends completely upon Christ. It must be a church that is totally committed, that is willing to sacrifice, that knows servant living, and lives in the presence, power and purpose of Christ. That takes time. We can learn the mechanics of cell life quickly. The dynamics of the process are more difficult. We must internalize a whole new set of church values and become part of a new church culture which operates out of an incarnational and transformational world view.

FAST FORWARD FROM A VALUE BASE

Some large churches seem to leap over the prototype phase, moving almost immediately into new cell church structures and impressive growth. Does this mean they have discovered some kind of special methods which enable them to bypass the prototyping and go immediately to multiplying? Not at all! Many churches transition quickly because a cell church *value base* has been laid in previous years. We must factor in this time of previous preparation.

This cell church value base is often built while still maintaining the appearance of a traditional church with many traditional structures. When these value based churches receive God's cell church vision, they have great potential for quickly transitioning into a cell church. If the vision and values are in place, the change process is dramatically accelerated.

The time these innovative churches used to change their vision and values is an essential element in their prototype period. They did not become instantaneous cell churches by changing structures. More than likely they have had a decade or more of their value base changing gradually, usually because of a strong leader who has had a long tenure with the church. That leader may have had no understanding of the cell church in the beginning. More than likely, the leader simply saw what he was doing as helping his church become more New Testament.

God prepared these churches to transition quickly, not because they found a shortcut around the prototype phase, but because they had already gone through some of the value changes that take place during the prototype phase.

INSTANT PUDDING

By the time church leaders arrive at one of our conferences many are beaten, bruised and battered by expectations of an instant operating cell church. They have sold their people on a relatively painless fast track to transition into a cell church. That expectation begins to crumble during the early stages of the process and, by the time they show up in a cell church conference, hope has turned to despair and desperation. To give proper credit, their disappointment has not destroyed the desire to be the New Testament cell church that God has placed in their heart. However, their faith is being severely tested by this process.

During the first day of teaching cell church seminars, I usually sense a lot of frustration and feelings of failure from leaders who have already begun their cell church journey. They have usually read a book, attended a seminar or visited some kind of church using small groups. All the wrong conclusions have been drawn about what it means for their church to transition into a cell church. They look for answers from each other without an understanding of guiding principles and values. This does serious damage. Deming commented about business people who get excited about quality control:

> Too often this is the story. The management of a company, seized with a desire to improve quality and productivity, knowing not how to go about it, having not guidance from principles, seeking

enlightenment, embark on excursions to other companies that are ostensibly doing well. They are received with open arms, and the exchange of ideas commences. They (visitors) learn what the host is doing, some of which may by accident be in accordance with the 14 points. Devoid of guiding principles, they are both adrift. Neither company knows whether or why any procedure is right, nor whether or why another is wrong. The question is not whether a business is successful, but why? And why was it not more successful? One can only hope that the visitors enjoy the ride. They are more to be pitied than censured.[3]

On the second day, I can almost predict the moment relief begins. During the session on the Prototype and Operational phases of the cell church the weight of becoming an instant cell church is lifted off their shoulders. As leaders begin to understand the cell church is not expected to come into existence full blown, there is almost an audible sigh of relief. Those attending the seminar have found it tremendously reassuring to finally realize that even Jesus proceeded through the prototype phase when developing His church. We can finally give up the unrealistic task of making instant cell church pudding!

17
JESUS' PROTOTYPE FACTORS

The Prototype acts as a buffer between
hypothesis and action.
—Michael Gerber

The 1995 Ford Contour and Mercury Mystique cost six billion dollars and several years to get into production. Can you believe that? Six *BILLION* dollars! Several years ago the Saturn was developed at a cost of three billion dollars. Evidently automobile companies feel a prototype model is essential for producing cars and are willing to spend the time and resources necessary to develop good working prototypes. This tedious and expensive process of prototyping requires vision, commitment and patience.

When Jesus came to begin His church, He first developed a prototype, a working model. This was His primary focus during the last three and a half years of ministry. He carefully put together all of the working parts of His church design and then physically returned to heaven before the church became operational. Today, churches desiring to be New Testament cell churches must go through the same prototype stage in order to reach their full potential as an operational cell church.

Certain cell church factors are handled differently during the prototype stage than at the point of full operation. Understanding these factors and implementing accordingly simplify the prototype process and strengthen the operational base. It will also speed up the time it takes to become a fully operational cell church. Remember—it is 50 times easier to get it right the first time!

The prototype and operational phases aren't different in nature and purpose. They are different in how they approach implementation. Because the prototype phase comes first and builds the foundation for the operational phase, it must approach strategy in a different way. The following factors are part of the prototype phase of cell church development:

1. TIME FACTOR

In the prototype phase, more time is required than in the operational phase to perform the same basic tasks. Some car prototype models may take months or even years to complete. Companies gladly allow those responsible for developing prototype to take the time and use the resources necessary to discover what will work and what will not work. However, if it takes as long to produce a car on the assembly line as in the prototype department, the company is in trouble. Spending time up front on the prototype allows eventual mass production.

The purpose of the cell church prototype is the same. It takes longer to do everything during the prototype phase because a model is being developed for duplication. Instant cell churches will not happen during the prototype phase. It takes a longer period of time to develop every part of the model. It takes:

- Longer to develop the initial leaders
- Longer to develop the cell community
- Longer to disciple a new believer
- Longer to reproduce and grow
- Longer to put into place the cell church infrastructure

Other church models may produce more numbers in the early stages. These include the seeker models, meta-church model and even some traditional church models. These other types of churches gather consumers and establish a distribution system pattern more quickly than the cell church model. However, they will have difficulty sustaining that growth, and most will fall behind the growth of a cell church. Once a cell church becomes operational exponential multiplication is possible because the prototype phase sets up a system through which all Christians are equipped and mobilized for ministry.

2. SKILL FACTOR

The Prototype phase requires more skilled workers. In the prototype phase, Ph.D.'s will get their hands greasy working to develop a new car so that less skilled workers will be able to do the same task in the operational phase. McDonald's has a system put into place by highly skilled entrepreneurs and innovators. This makes it possible for the less skilled workers to eventually run the business.

Jesus' strategy was for His church system to work with the less skilled workers. Jesus began His cell church with men who could become visionary leaders. They were trained during the prototype phase. In 1 Corinthians 1:26-29 Paul stated this principle:

> For consider your calling, brethren, that there were not many wise according to the flesh, not many mighty, not many noble; but God has chosen the foolish things of the world to shame the wise, and God has chosen the weak things of the world to shame the things which are strong, and the base things of the world and the despised, God has chosen, the things that are not, that He might nullify the things that are.

The traditional one-winged church is dependent upon highly professional and skilled leaders to do the work of the ministry. Jesus' system releases and empowers *all* of us to participate in the most important tasks of a believer: making disciples as we love God, our neighbor, and each other.

3. LEADERSHIP FACTOR

Jesus focused on leadership during the Prototype phase. Coleman writes, "His concern was not with programs to reach the multitudes, but with men whom the multitudes would follow. . . . Men were to be His method of bringing the world to God."[2]

I recently talked with the staff of a large church with a vision to become a pure cell church. The only exception was the senior pastor of the church. He was preoccupied with a heavy schedule of outside speaking engagements. He saw cells as one more attachment to the many church activities. He felt someone on the staff could oversee them. The staff members asked me, "Must our senior pastor be involved in cell life if we are to become a cell church?"

That question is like a pastor asking a pulpit committee from a traditional church, "Must I be involved in Sunday worship?" Of course he must! Sunday worship is the primary part of the life of the traditional church.

"Must the senior pastor be directly engaged in the transition into cells?" How could it be any other way? Cell life is the basic experience of the church. If senior leaders are detached from the prototype process, they will not be able to give leadership at the operational phase. The most skilled leaders must participate in discovering and implementing the basic system. This includes the senior pastor and key leadership of the church.

Delegation is an important principle in the cell church. Cell churches thrive because they have a Jethro leadership system through which leadership is delegated to leaders over *10's, 50's, 100's* and *1000's*. But vision and example can't be delegated! Senior church leaders must cast the vision and set the example of living in basic Christian community during the prototype phase. The senior leader must model the community he is expecting everyone else to live in. If leaders don't have the time to live together in cell life, how can they expect members to do it? After they have walked through the prototype stage and the church moves into the operational stage, visionary leaders have the lifestyle and experience which gives them the ability to lead from within the system itself.

Jesus' continuum during the prototype phase is a leadership process. This starts with the most senior of leadership and leaders are added to leaders in an incremental process of larger and larger leadership units, as follows:

- The visionary team
- An inner circle of twelve core leaders
- A support network of up to 70 committed followers
- 120 - 200 Base Congregation

4. EVANGELISM FACTOR

What kind of evangelism should take place out in the world during the prototype phase? How does prototype evangelism differ from operational evangelism? Certainly the difference is not in passion or commitment. It may, however, differ in focus and target. The prototype phase is an important time to lay the foundation for future exponential evangelism, through:

1. Developing a passion for evangelism that overflows from edification
2. Establishing a cell system through which unbelievers can be contacted, birthed, nurtured and trained
3. Training members to engage in holistic evangelism: relationship evangelism, seeker evangelism and evangelism to hard-core unbelievers
4. Eliminating program barriers to evangelism
5. Balancing event evangelism with the development of cell infrastructure

Evangelism that reaches friends, relatives and acquaintances within one's sphere of influence (called *oikos* evangelism) works best during the prototype phase for the following reasons:

1. *Oikos* evangelism teaches the most basic method for reaching people.
2. *Oikos* evangelism fits into a newly forming community and is least disruptive.
3. *Oikos* evangelism builds a broad network for future harvest while the cell community is being formed.
4. *Oikos* evangelism helps control the number of dysfunctional people who are brought into the cell during the critical time of establishing community.
5. *Oikos* evangelism trains cell members to win both the responsive seeker and hardcore unbelievers.

Large event evangelism can occur during the prototype period, but only at carefully selected times. Large evangelism events without a cell base can be time consuming, disruptive of cell life, and may require high maintenance during a time when developing the cell infrastructure should be the priority.

What kind of evangelism should take place in the cell meetings during the prototype phase? The same kind of evangelism that should be happening in the cell meetings during the operational phase. The type of evangelism described in 1 Corinthians 14:24-25 should be practiced:

But if all prophesy, and an unbeliever or an ungifted man enters, he is convicted by all, he is called to account by all; the secrets of his heart are disclosed; and so he will fall on his face and worship God, declaring that God is certainly among you.

This is *the presence of the Lord* evangelism. Unbelievers who come into the cell group should be exposed to the presence of Christ. The meeting format should not be changed to convert them or to focus on them. They should be allowed to sit and watch God at work in His people. That is the greatest witness on the face of the earth. We often assume a verbal exchange of information is the most potent witness to unbelievers. The New Testament church knew the most powerful witness was the community of believers living in the presence, power and purpose of Christ.

It is not Christian perfection and certainly not the lost nature of the visitor that is showcased in a cell meeting, but the presence of Christ. Through the imperfection of Christians, God reveals His power to those who observe. When unbelievers attend a cell, it is a time for Christ to witness, not for every Christian to verbally witness.

In our first small group experience in Thailand, I learned how not to do evangelism in a cell. We started a Friday night group in our home after completing our first year of language school. We were experiencing true fellowship and edification, with a lot of singing and sharing. One Friday evening, a member brought a man he met in the market with whom he had engaged in heated debate about Christianity and Buddhism. The Christian said, "Come to our meeting, and you will find out what Christianity is all about."

That night the meal and singing went well. The Christians and the lost man engaged in cordial and courteous conversation. However, when the formal meeting started, things heated up. The format of ministry to one another and listening to God was quickly abandoned. The Christians, from the oldest to the newest, had been carefully loading their "witnessing guns" while we were eating and singing. When the unbeliever began to question and argue, everyone took out their witnessing guns, aimed and fired at him during the remaining part of the meeting. He was shot full of holes. He never came back to another meeting, and I don't blame him. I would not have returned either.

What our evangelism approach did to that lost man was bad enough, but even more tragic and damaging was what it did to the group of

Christians. Before the lost man showed up, Christ was edifying the body. Lives were being changed. When the lost man came into the group, it ceased to focus on Christ and turned its attention to the lost man. The nature of the cell changed. Christ was not able to edify the Christians and strengthen their lives. The conversion of this one man became the focus of the meeting, not Christ. Edification therefore was short-circuited. What that unconverted Buddhist man needed was to meet Christ, not to become engaged in intellectual arguments. The group should have continued focusing on Christ so the man could see Christ at work in the midst of His people. Perhaps, he would have fallen on his face and have said, "Surely God is in this place."

Ralph Neighbour shares what happened in a cell group session where the focus remained on Christ even though two unbelievers were present. This is the way evangelism ought to happen during the cell meeting. One of the unbelievers was a banker with a Catholic background who had not attended church in years. He had recently received a note from his wife telling him she had walked out of their marriage. He was hurting!

That night, Christ ministered to the needs of several other people while the unbeliever, from an unthreatened position, observed God at work in the group. Later this distraught unbeliever accepted the Lord. Dr. Neighbour interprets for us what happened there:

> Do you understand? The evangelism 'method' in that meeting was the presence of the Lord operating through His Bride! He was 'convicted by all; called to account by all; the secrets of his heart was poured out;' and he almost literally fell on his face as the men prayed together on those stairs. He had discovered God was certainly among the people in the cell![2]

During the prototype stage, evangelism beyond the cell group meetings must also be a priority. The man who showed up for the cell meeting described above had first been contacted through a group designed to contact and cultivate unbelievers. He was then invited to the cell where the focus was on Christ, not the lost.

Only a mature cell, with a clear understanding of its purpose, will keep its focus on Christ when unbelievers are in attendance. If in every meeting, the focus changes from edification to evangelism because an outsider attends, continuity and community is lost. Let the weak Christians be nurtured. Let the body be healed. Let members be delivered from strongholds. Let the believers as well as unbeliever meet Christ in the midst!

The prototype phase is a time to lay the foundation for future exponential evangelism. During the prototype phase, Jesus taught about evangelism, modeled evangelism, trained His disciples to evangelize by sending them out two by two and cast the vision for evangelism. All of this was done within a cell community context. During the prototype period, however, He never allowed the evangelizing of the masses to interfere with His primary purpose of equipping leaders and establishing His community system.

5. EDIFICATION FACTOR

During the prototype phase, cell members must learn how to edify and build up one another. Jesus designed the church to evangelize from a healthy edification base where believers become channels for edification. Only an edifying church will be an effective evangelizing church. Ray Stedman recognized the importance of evangelizing from a healthy body. "A healthy body is necessary to do effective work. To attempt evangelism while the body of Christ is sick and ailing is worse than useless."[3] E. Stanley Jones illustrated the danger of not building up one another. In *The Way*, he wrote:

> I sat alongside of Lake Massaweepie, in the Adirondacks, writing this book. Each morning a wild duck came by foraging near the shore with her brood. One duck seemed to be weaker than the rest and spent most of his time just keeping up with the others. He had no time to feed. Many of us spend most of our time keeping up with our tasks. We have no time to feed our inner spirits. We lack a plus, a margin of power that lets us meet our tasks with something left over.[4]

This weak little duck needed a place it could feed without trying to keep up with the others. It needed a flock that cared for the weaker and did not gauge its feeding time to accommodate the speed of the strongest. To continue to try to keep up without an opportunity to feed dooms the weak little duck to become weaker and weaker.

All of us are weak little ducks. Every Christian needs a time of personal feeding that is not tied to keeping up with the activity of the crowd. Without this, the Christian grows weaker and weaker. The cell group is the context in which we receive a "plus, a margin of power that lets us meet our tasks with something left over."

This is the reason the basic Christian community must be, first of all, a time of edification. The cell group must be a time when every little duck can be fed without the pressure of trying to keep up. As the pattern of edification is established during the prototype stage, the groups are then prepared to move into the expansion of ministry and evangelism during the operational stage.

6. Equipping Factor

During the three and a half years of prototype development, Jesus continually made the choice to concentrate on equipping leaders. Great crowds followed Him, and yet He seemed almost distracted and detached from the crowds, choosing rather to spend as much time as possible with individuals and especially with His leaders.

Jesus even ran away from the crowds. He got in a boat and went across the Sea of Galilee. He took His disciples and went up into the mountains. "Jesus did not want anyone to know where he was, because he was teaching his disciples" (Mark 9:30) (NIV).

Some suggest Jesus tried to separate Himself from the crowds because He was personally weary and needed rest. His weariness of body may have been part of it, but that was not the primary reason Jesus tried to distance Himself from the crowds. Jesus was focused on equipping a *leadership core* during the prototype phase. Focusing on the multitudes during the beginning stages could have kept Him from eventually reaching the multitudes.

The prototype period is the time to equip leaders and to establish an equipping track. Every member will be developed as a disciple within the context of a systematic equipping track. The equipping track functions with self-study, with a sponsor and within a cell context.

In China, ducks and geese are force-fed. Maize and corn are poured down their throats with a funnel. Ducks and geese grow very large with this feeding approach. However, if this method is changed, they will die even if food is all around them. Force-fed ducks and geese lack the ability to feed themselves. Nothing is more important than discovering and implementing an effective equipping track which will teach every new member how to feed without dependence.

It is critical that the equipping track be developed, tested and incorporated into the cell church during the prototype period. Without an effective equipping track interns will not be developed and new Christians will continue to be part of the problem instead of part of the solution. It is essential that this equipping track be completed before dramatic growth kicks in. After growth and multiplication begins, it is very difficult to go back and develop an effective equipping track, much less go back and catch up on equipping all those who came in without being equipped in the first place. The initial cycles of a cell church provide an opportunity to develop an equipping system through which future evangelistic exponential multiplication can be conserved in exponential equipping methods.

7. REORGANIZING FACTOR

The prototype stage is a time when cells can be reorganized and rearranged in order to develop several healthy prototype models. It is overly optimistic to expect all cells to multiply every six to nine months while learning how cells and community function. A church must test out cell life when it is beginning its process. The pressure to multiply must become secondary to learning how to do cells and live together in community. It is therefore more important to strengthen the first cells by rearranging the people in them than multiplying out weak and dysfunctional cells in order to keep up an arbitrary growth rate. If a cell church is under pressure from the start to multiply exponentially, little time is left for developing leaders and infrastructure necessary to sustain exponential multiplication.

Factors for reorganizing during the Prototype phase may include one or a combination of the following:

- Reorganize around leaders
- Reorganize geographically
- Reorganize in order to develop congregational community and vision
- Reorganize in order to prune and pull up flawed and sick cells
- Reorganize to keep groups from becoming ingrown and stagnant
- Reorganize in order to assimilate new leaders into the mix

During the prototype stage, identify and strengthen healthy cells that will multiply. Reorganize unhealthy cells. For example: five cells may become seven or eight cells instead of ten cells. After another cycle, the seven cells may become ten cells instead of doubling to fourteen. At a certain point, every cell should be expected to multiply during a normal cell cycle, but that normal cell cycle must be set after the church has become fully operational.

The length of a cell cycle may vary from place to place. Typically, it will require from four months to a year for multiplication to take place. If a cell won't, or can't, multiply in a year, something is wrong with the basic structure of the cell. The group should be reorganized by distributing members into other healthy groups.

How many cell cycles are required before true multiplication can take place in a cell church? It depends on the condition of the original cells. How effective are the cell leaders? Do the cells have interns? Is an equipping track in place? How many dysfunctional people are in the cells? Are the cells operating as task groups or around the person, power and purpose of Christ? Are the groups experiencing real New Testament community and body life? Do the members of the cells know how to edify and minister to each other? Has a cell church value base been internalized?

During the prototype phase, several cell cycles of six to eight months each are probably required before cells can be established that have a reasonable hope of multiplying exponentially.

8. Predictability Factor

During the prototype phase, predictable patterns of cell life must be established. Some kind of consistent framework is necessary which can be duplicated in each succeeding cycle. The following four aspects of a cell church must operate with predictability and constancy of purpose: cell life, equipping, evangelism and leadership. Without predictability in these areas, leaders can't be trained, and without leaders, exponential multiplication is impossible.

If every cell leader does "what is right in his own eyes," no set pattern will exist by which future leaders can be trained and materials developed. Suppose you have five cells with three different cell formats, three different ways of equipping new members, different approaches to evangelism and several ways of choosing and operating as leaders. What will your prototype look like after the fourth or fifth generation of multiplication? It would be chaotic! Every multiplying cycle will be more diverse and incompatible. The cells will be so different that interchanging leaders, materials and methods will be out of the question.

When we hear the words "predictability" and "constancy of purpose," we often think "control" and "loss of freedom." Some may ask, "If every cell follows the same format, materials and tracks, doesn't this limit the work of the Holy Spirit? Isn't this just another cookie cutter approach to church life?" This is not so! Our danger today is the lack of a predictable framework. Constant change only gives the illusion of progress and freedom.

When I was a senior in high school, the school hired a new basketball coach. He immediately started installing a new offense. We only had seven or eight basic plays, but we ran them over and over again in practice. The point guard would throw the ball into the center and then go screen for the forward who would break for the basket and shoot. Without any opposition, we scored every time. However, in a game situation the defense did not always cooperate. Therefore, we had to be creative. However, since we had the basic plays, we could always fall back on a system that gave stability.

Having a set cell format, along with standard tracks for equipping, evangelism and leadership does not restrict but releases the work of the Holy Spirit. Test cycles during the prototype stage give a way to establish a framework in which effective Christian living can take place. The prototype period allows leaders to discover and define the predictable parts of the cell church.

Strategic Phases	Schaller's Change Process	New Testament Numbers	Jesus' Continuum	Vision Action
Preparation	Convergence	Prophetic Word (Jesus)	Cell Church Vision	Conceiv
P R O T O T Y P E	Initiating Set	2-3 people	Innovation	Introduced
	Legitimating Sponsorship	12 people	Core Leadership	Owned
	Execution Set	**70 people**	**Support Network**	**Implemented**
Critical Mass / O P E R A T I O N A L	Fulfillment of Charter	120 people	Base Congregation	Empowered
		3000-5000	Church Expansion	Expanded

18

JESUS' LEADERSHIP STRATEGY

One must decide where he wants his ministry to
count . . . in the momentary applause of popular
recognition or in the reproduction of his life in
a few chosen men who will carry on his
work after he has gone.
—Robert Coleman

In John 17, Jesus reported to the Father that their strategy was going to be successful. Why was Jesus optimistic about this? He was facing the cross, the betrayal of Judas and the falling away of the disciples. What was the basis of his confidence? Consider three possible reports Jesus could have presented:

Report Number 1: Our strategy will work because within the first year huge crowds were following Me. I could not get away from them. They clamored for me to speak to them and even left their homes and jobs to hear Me preach. There was great response and popularity.

Report Number 2: The strategy will work because in the near future, Pentecost will take place. Thousands are going to believe during just one week of time. Therefore, the strategy will work because of the large number of believers who will exist after Pentecost.

Report Number 3: The strategy will work because of the core disciples. These are the ones who have lived with me in community. I have taught them and lived with them. They know I have come from You, Father! Our strategy will work because of these leaders.

Which report sounds most promising and logical? In light of many traditional church growth methods, Report one or two would appear to have the best chance of success. Both reports have sufficient numbers either at the beginning or the end of the process to forecast expectations of success.

However, Jesus confidently gave the *third* report to the Father. Jesus had a leadership strategy, not a crowd strategy or a numbers strategy. Over the past several decades, Robert Coleman has been one of the clearest voices trumpeting the importance of Jesus' leadership strategy. He says, "Leadership was the emphasis. Jesus had already demonstrated by His own ministry that the deluded masses were ripe for the harvest, but without spiritual shepherds to lead them, how could they ever be won?"[1]

Coleman also observes:

What good would it have been for His ultimate objective to arouse the masses to follow Him if these people had no subsequent supervision nor instruction in the Way? It had been demonstrated on numbers of occasions that the crowd was an easy prey to false gods when left without proper care. . . . For this reason, unless Jesus' converts were given competent men of God to lead them on and protect them in the truth they would soon fall into confusion and despair, and the last state would be worse then the first. Thus, before the world could ever be permanently helped, men would have to be raised up who could lead the multitudes in the things of God.[2]

JESUS PREPARED THE DISCIPLES IN A SPECIAL LEADERSHIP FRAMEWORK

Notice the leadership triangle in Figure 6. At the top of the triangle is Christ, the catalyst or innovator. At the second level of the triangle is the inner circle Peter, James and John. On the base line of the triangle are the remaining nine members of Jesus' core leaders. The extended family members are around this core group.

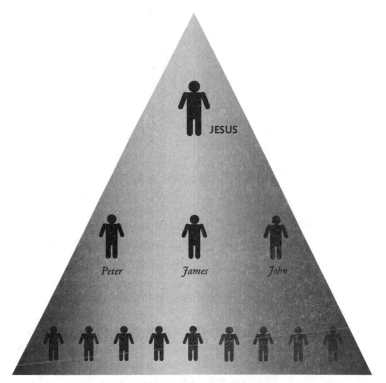

Figure 6. Jesus' Leadership Structure

In this leadership context, Jesus related to His leaders in several ways. At times, He related with them one on one, as He did with Peter, Thomas, John, Phillip and even Judas. He also related to the twelve as a unit. Much of His teaching was to the Twelve; He often took them away from the crowds in order to be with them. In a study of the Gospel of Mark, Jim Egli has suggested that 49% of Mark is given to the time Jesus spent with His disciples.[3] Coleman adds,

> One cannot help but observe in this connection that the references to "the disciples" as a corporate body are much more frequent in the Gospels than are references to an individual disciple. . . . When it is remembered that these accounts were written under inspiration by the disciples, and not Jesus, it is quite significant that they would set forth their own place in such terms. We need not infer from this that the disciples were unimportant as

individuals, for such was not the case, but it does impress us with the fact that the disciples understood their Lord to look upon them as a body of believers being trained together for a common mission. They saw themselves through Christ first as a church, and secondly as individuals within that body.[4]

The disciples related to each other on a one to one basis. Sometimes these relationships were not good. For instance, as they moved toward Jerusalem for the last time, they were upset with each other. James, John and their mother were trying to gain advantage over the rest. Jesus' leadership triangle allowed personal contact with each other, both good and bad. This approach to leadership provided Jesus with many teachable moments to instruct, encourage and admonish His disciples.

Jesus also frequently related to the three in His inner circle. He took Peter, James and John with Him to the Mount of Transfiguration. When He healed the daughter of Jarius, Peter, James and John also entered the room with Him while the others remained outside. Coleman notes:

> Within the select apostolic group Peter, James and John seemed to enjoy a more special relationship to the Master than did the other nine . . . So noticeable is the preference given to these three that had it not been for the incarnation of selflessness in the Person of Christ it could well have precipitated feelings of resentment on the part of the other apostles. The fact that there is no record of the disciples complaining about the pre-eminence of the three, though they did murmur about other things, is proof that where preference is shown in the right spirit and for the right reason offense need not arise.[5]

The last time Jesus was with His disciples before His death was in the Garden of Gethsemane. There, He physically arranged the disciples in this leadership framework. He left the nine at the outermost point, took the three inner circle of Peter, James and John in deeper with Him. Then He went further into the Garden. On the last night He was with them, Jesus modeled how He had been relating to His leaders for the past three years.

SUBGROUPS IN THE TWELVE

At least one other possible relationship exists within the context of Jesus' leadership triangle. Peter, James and John could have also related in a mentor role to three others. These *sub-groups* within the twelve would allow the inner circle to model Jesus' relationship with them to three others.

Subgroups within the broader twelve would allow transference of leadership found in 2 Timothy 2:2 to operate in Jesus' leadership framework: "And the things which you have heard from me in the presence of many witnesses, these entrust to faithful men, who will be able to teach others also." The leader should always train other leaders to duplicate what he has learned. Jesus did this within a community of twelve.

USING THE TRIANGLE

Over the past several years, I have consulted with churches of all types and sizes about transitioning into a cell church. I have yet to come across a church where this leadership triangle did not fit. During this leadership stage in the prototype process you will:

1. Discover the format and dynamic of the basic cell unit.
2. Test out the essential working parts of a cell church.
3. Identify and gather essential leaders.
4. Develop a cell infrastructure.

1. DISCOVER THE FORMAT AND DYNAMIC OF THE BASIC CELL UNIT

One of the most important tasks for a fledgling cell church is discovering what the basic building block, the cell, looks like. Jesus' leadership triangle can help us do that, Figure 7. The effectiveness of a cell church depends upon the basic cell unit. Every church must discover how God wants to be *Lord* in their cell groups every time they meet in a way that can be repeated to the tenth multiplication. A pastor and his innovators can discover the characteristics of the basic cell unit by using the leadership triangle.

First, a pastor chooses a Peter, James and John as his innovators. In an existing church, these leaders will already be functioning in some kind of leadership capacity. In a new start, these leaders should be part of the church planting team. They, along with their spouses, form a basic Christian community of eight persons. In the case of an unmarried leader, another single person can be added to the group. When forming youth or college leadership cells, eight student leaders can be chosen for the initial modeling process (Don't get hung up on the number "eight." The

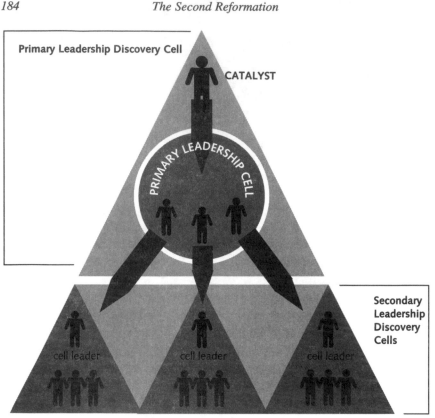

Figure 7. Using the Triangle

discovery group may consist of six to ten persons.) The objectives of the initial leadership discovery cell is to:

- Live together in community
- Take off relational masks
- Learn the meaning of edification
- Discover a workable cell format
- Experience the dynamic of cell life
- Nurture a passion for evangelism

This leadership discovery cell should experience community, not study how a cell works. Getting together to talk about cell church principles should be reserved for another type of meeting. This group must experience the most basic and essential body life of a cell church. If leaders in a church have not experienced community, fellowship and edification, then how will the members know what should happen in a cell?

This initial leadership discovery cell may last only a few months. It can be accelerated by having frequent intensive times together, including weekend retreats or one day meetings. The intent is not only to experience every part of cell life but to discover the *presence, power* and *purpose* of the basic cell and to determine the format appropriate for future cell meetings.

A church cannot learn cell life second hand, from experiences of other churches or books. To understand cell life, leaders must personally experience a cell. Deming said, "It is a hazard to copy. It is necessary to understand the theory of what one wishes to do or to make."[6] Leaders who copy the basic cell structure from someone else do so at the peril of their church. Cell life must be from the original, not copied from others. Only God has the original. (Refer to chapter 13 to see a basic cell pattern that can help you begin this process.)

The ultimate test of leadership is not whether a person can lead, but whether that person can teach others to lead in the same way. After the first leadership discovery cell cycle of two or three months, the leaders should form the secondary leadership discovery cells. It is possible that the first leadership discovery cell worked because the leader was highly skilled. Therefore, the leader should restructure the original leadership discovery cell into three new cells. "Peter" is assigned three more leaders, "James" is given three and "John" also has a group with three new leaders. Again, along with their spouses, they experience the mechanics and dynamics of the kind of cell they want to form in the church. The second discovery cell cycle begins with the cell pattern which has grown out of the experience of the original leadership discovery cell. The person who led the initial leadership discovery cell should give oversight to the three leadership discovery cells.

The purpose is to fine-tune the format and dynamic cell life already experienced by the first leadership discovery cell. After another discovery cycle of two to three months, all involved in these leadership discovery cells should have experienced cell life.

2. TEST OUT THE ESSENTIAL WORKING PARTS OF A CELL CHURCH

The first working cell units may now be formed with selected church members. Leaders who have already experienced cell life in one of the leadership discovery cells are the cell leaders, interns and core members of the new *Test Cells*. Additional committed church members are brought in to be the remaining members of the cells. They can include up to eight adults. At this important prototype phase, it is better to have a few strong cells than many weak ones. The number of test cells formed depends upon the size of the church. However, it is important to remember these are test cells. This is not yet the time to include the entire church membership in cells. Forming five cells as a test group is effective and can serve as a valid control group for the first cycle in a church of almost any size.

The test cells will use the same mechanics and dynamics discovered by the leaders during the two discovery cycles. However, these test cells will be different in some ways from the discovery cell. First, these test cells will stay together for a full cell cycle of six to nine months, whereas the two preceeding discovery cell cycles, were only two or three months. Second, these cells are different because they will reach out to their *oikoses* (relationships) and grow by adding converts as well as periodically adding existing church members.

As these test cells move toward the end of their six to nine month cycle, they should be reorganized rather than multiplied. (See the Reorganizing Factor in chapter 17.) Reorganization rather than multiplication is preferred at this time because most of these early cells will still not function as operational cells will function. They are learning how to do evangelism, how to equip, how to edify, how to lead, how to develop an intern and how to be accountable to each other. In addition to these important elements, these groups are also trying to experience community and learn how to deal with dysfunctional members. During the test cycles, members in existing cells must be rearranged and reassigned in order to develop several strong and healthy cell prototypes.

As leaders process through the discovery cell cycles and the test cell cycles, they must also implement the essential working parts of the cell church. A cell church will not work without establishing an equipping track, evangelism overflow, intern training, balanced celebration worship, a prayer base and a leadership structure.

These working parts are interdependent. For instance, it is difficult to train leaders until the equipping track is working. Without the leadership structure, evangelism will not be effective. At first, as these working parts are being inserted, the output from cell life will seem slow. However, as each part becomes more efficient, it releases elements of the other components to operate at a higher level. Synergism begins to operate as the different working parts complement each other.

An *equipping track* must be established through which every member of the church can be equipped for effective and productive Christian living. During the leadership discovery cycles and test cell cycles, a systematic equipping track must be developed, tested and inserted into cell life. A cell church will not function without a way to develop every member into a productive disciple. Several test cycles give a controlled environment to test and layout an effective equipping track.

Evangelism must begin to overflow from cell life through natural relationship. New believers are brought into meaningful cell life to be nurtured into productive disciples. During the test cycles, cells learn friendship evangelism as a natural part of cell life. Cells begin to contact unbelievers at three points. First, cells target unbelievers who are already part of the member's sphere of influence. Second, cells welcome and incorporate unbelievers who come seeking Christ and community. Third, cell members contact hardcore unbelievers by meeting their felt needs.

Intern training must be established in the test cycle stage. A cell church grows because it produces intern leaders for every level of leadership. Interns are the key to growth. Leaders must learn how to use on-the-job training to develop cell interns who effectively do what the cell leader has modeled. Intern training should include structured learning, using a systematic curriculum and on-the-job training guided by the cell leader.

During the initial cell models a *leadership structure* must be set up and tested. As you develop test cells, you will need to establish the oversight structure so that leaders can learn how to function over 50's and 100's and 1000's (see Figure 8, page 188).

As you experience cell life, celebration worship will have new meaning. Meeting God together will be an overflow of meeting God in the cell groups. Prayer will also need to be built underneath all that is done. Without a vital dependence on the Father, nothing will be accomplished.

During the discovery and test cycles these essential components must be developed and built into the structure and life of the church.

3. IDENTIFYING AND GATHERING ESSENTIAL LEADERS

The leadership triangle sets into motion the development of a Jethro leadership structure that provides oversight at levels of 1000's, 100's, 50's and 10's. Cell churches usually have a leadership to member ratio of

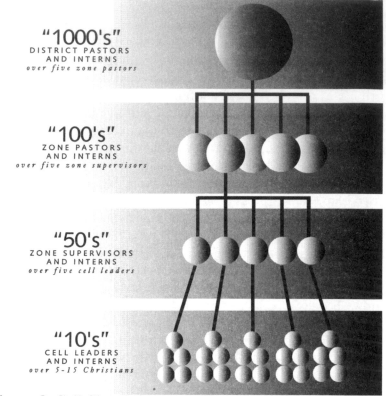

Figure 8. Cell Church Structure (The Jethro Structure)

one leader for every five to ten members. This may vary to some degree, but the principle of leadership in a cell church is to oversee members within a small group context.

Figure 8 illustrates several important characteristics of leadership in a cell church:

1. Leadership is organized around four types of leaders who can be identified by the number of members they serve. Leaders are responsible for 10's, 50's, 100's and 1000's. These numbers are flexible categories, not rigid barriers. The categories have a low and high range in order to allow for growth. For instance the person serving as a leader of 50's (Zone Supervisors) may actually oversee two to six cells or twenty to sixty persons. Those serving as a leader of 100's (Zone Pastors) may care for ten to twenty-five cells or one hundred to three hundred persons.

2. Leaders are linked to each other for support and accountability. For instance, a leader supporting 10's (Cell Leader) is linked for support to a leader over 50's. The leader over 50's is linked to a leader over 100's and those over 100's to a leader over 1000's (District Pastor).

3. Interns are assigned to every level of leadership, including 1000's, 100's, 50's and 10's. These interns are the future growth of your groups. Without them, it will be impossible to multiply and grow.

4. Leaders of 1000's and 100's are usually salaried full-time leaders. Leaders of 50's and 10's are volunteer members who are not paid. The possibility of exponential multiplication is compromised if salaries must be paid to cell leaders and those who minister to 50's.

5. The profile for the cell leader overseeing 10 people should be Aquila or Priscilla, not Paul or Timothy. Exponential multiplication will be impossible if the cell leader over 10's is seen as an ordained position.

6. The qualifications for leaders listed in 1 Timothy 3 and Titus 1 normally is used to describe the leader of 50's who is in an overseeing role. Cell leaders at the 10's level must be seen as servants and not as leaders subject to more rigid qualifications.

7. Leadership in a cell church is predicated upon servanthood. Philippians 2:5-11 is one of the most important passages for cell church leaders. Leaders cannot be those who desire to climb the leadership ladder. They must operate with a servant heart, as modeled by Jesus in the upper room when He took a towel and basin and washed the disciples' feet.

8. In an operational cell church, leaders move vertically through the system instead of horizontally by being brought in from the outside. This leadership system allows a leader to be trained in his own church to enter into every stage of leadership.

9. In a fully operational cell church, the Jethro leadership structure provides a fail-safe system for leaders to prove themselves in the basic leadership roles before assuming greater responsibilities. This on-the-job training provides a context in which to identify doctrinal or character defects. Unqualified leaders can be identified early in the process and be gently removed or given more training.

10. The most important leadership role is the cell leader. All other leaders exist to facilitate and support what is happening at the cell level.

11. This leadership structure provides a context in which Ephesians 4:12 can function. Leaders provided by God equip the saints for the work of ministry at the most basic level of cell life.

Figure 9. Developing Infrastructure

As a team of leaders moves through the discovery cell cycles and the test cell cycles, this unique leadership structure must be tested out and put into place.

4. DEVELOP A CELL INFRASTRUCTURE

The leadership triangle is the first part of the process of developing a cell infrastructure which eventually becomes the base congregation. Figure 9 gives a big picture of what is happening during the process described in this chapter. Notice how the leadership triangle relates to the broader cell infrastructure that is developing during the prototype. In a cell church, all activities and components are connected to the cell infrastructure.

As the above graphic illustrates, building the prototype begins with the leadership triangle. During the two initial leadership discovery cycles, senior leaders develop the dynamics and mechanics of life in basic Christian community. When the leaders have discovered how God wants to live in their midst, in His presence, power and purpose, in community life, the leaders form the first test cycle. The circles in the chart represent a series of test cycles. The test cycle may number up to three or four cycles of six to nine months. This means the test cycle phase could last as long as two years or more.

The goal of the test cycle phase is to develop several healthy cells, establish the leadership structure and learn how to equip, evangelize and train interns. Other members are brought into the new test cells at each cycle when the old test cells are reorganized and new ones are added. The goal is to eventually have ten to fifteen healthy cells which serve as the remnant model to transition the entire church.

When ten to fifteen healthy cells are functioning, the process of internalizing cell life into the total church body is begun. The church body is prepared for this internal change by the senior pastor who casts the vision and helps members internalize cell church values. Some structures should be streamlined in this process in order to prepare for the introduction of cells to the entire church body. A larger and larger number of the leadership of the church will become part of the leadership vision: twelve will compose the leadership core, seventy will form the support network and finally one hundred and twenty will become the base congregation. This process took three and a half years for Jesus. A typical church will need three to five years to complete the prototype process.

Moving to a point of introducing cells into the broad church structure will take at least two years. That much time is needed to learn the mechanics and dynamics of cell church life. The cell infrastructure and the installation of an equipping track, evangelism, intern training, celebration worship, prayer, and leadership structure must be set into place. In addition, God must prepare the leadership to live in this kind of church. Both of these take time.The final stages of this process are described in greater detail in chapter twenty.

Jesus had a leadership strategy and so must we. The leadership triangle gives a framework to develop and implement the initial leadership strategy necessary for becoming an operational cell church.

Strategic Phases	Schaller's Change Process	New Testament Numbers	Jesus' Continuum	Vision Action
Preparation	Convergence	*Prophetic Word (Jesus)*	Cell Church Vision	*Conceived*
PROTOTYPE	**Initiating Set**	**2-3 people**	**Innovation**	**Introduced**
	Legitimating Sponsorship	**12 people**	**Core Leadership**	**Owned**
	Execution Set	70 people	Support Network	Implemented
Critical Mass / OPERATIONAL	Fulfillment of Charter	120 people	Base Congregation	Empowered
		3000-5000	Church Expansion	Expanded

19

JESUS' SUPPORT NETWORK

*But if a paradigm is ever to triumph it must gain
some first supporters, men who will develop it to the
point where hardheaded arguments can be
produced and multiplied.*
—Thomas Kuhn

H ave you ever been on a runaway horse? I have. My first horse, Judy, was a pretty little sorrel mare with a blaze face and three stocking feet. However, she was not as sweet as her name or appearance! When Judy tired, she wanted to go home to the barn. As a ten year old, I didn't have the strength to convince her she needed to stay out in the hot sun carrying me to my next adventure. When Judy took the bit and headed home, I had two choices: either hang on until she decided to stop, or look for soft sand, and bail off.

Jesus' support network of seventy must have felt like that as they followed Him to Jerusalem for the final time. They had tried to turn His face away from Jerusalem. They had heard the plots, seen the increasing anger and hate in the faces of the Jewish leaders and sensed the apprehension of Rome. No matter how hard they tried, they could not turn Him.

Makeup of Jesus' Support Network

Jesus' support network was made up of several groups of leaders who related to each other around a common vision. This group included the twelve whom Christ chose as His special small group. The immediate families of the twelve were also part of the support network, along with their extended families such as John Mark whose mother, Mary, was one of the followers. Many of the early support network were disciples of John the Baptist. The women were frequently mentioned as loyal supporters who related to Jesus in a special way. A portion of Jesus' family was also part of the support network. His mother, Mary, is always seen in a support role to Jesus, even though some of Jesus' earthly brothers and sisters questioned His intentions. This tight network of followers was absolutely essential to the development of His movement.

SIX ELEMENTS IN THE SUPPORT NETWORK

Lyle Schaller lists the following six essential elements found in an effective support group. When one is able to convert Schaller's language to the New Testament events, it becomes obvious Jesus was following these same universal principles in developing the first church. Notice the final step of ownership. The support network owns the idea and actually implements the concept. Until a new idea draws a committed support network around it, there will be no significant implementation of the idea.

NUMBERS *There must be sufficient numbers in the support group to accomplish the stated goal.*

LEGITIMATION *This is a "stamp of approval" that is essential to gain other required support.*

LOYALTY *The importance of loyalty is often overlooked in the efforts to develop a support group. Its value is most visible in its absence.*

SKILL *Skilled leadership is necessary first to gain the necessary approval of the proposed change and then to make the change an operational reality.*

COALITION *The ability to accept different ideas about how to implement change and to include others and their ideas in the process.*

OWNERSHIP *The capability of a support group to take an idea from a smaller initiating group and to adopt it as "ours!"* [1]

A support network is essential in the process of beginning a new cell church or to transition an existing church into a cell church. In the case of a new start, the work will grow by gathering up to seventy committed followers who are willing to implement the strategy. In a transitioning church, if seventy members are not willing to commit to the vision wholeheartedly, there is little hope of transitioning the entire church member-ship. The support network of seventy also forms the important test cells in the process of developing the church.

"Let's Go and Die With Him."

A support network of seventy battle-tested followers will exhibit a special attitude and commitment toward the task. Immediately following the death of Lazarus, the disciples realized that Jesus couldn't be turned from Jerusalem, Thomas spoke their heart: "Well, let's go and die with Him!" (John 11:16).

Jesus' support network did not understand all He was doing. They did not agree with his decision. They feared where He was leading them, but they were so committed they would face death with Him in Jerusalem.

The support network is loyal and will move into personal danger in order to follow the vision. Granted, they scattered like a covey of quail after they arrived in Jerusalem for Passover, but they went into uncertainty and danger with Him.

Fred and Peggy have been with us in Houston from the first year of our church plant. Fred admitted he had always been a "runner." When confrontation started in a church or things got difficult, Fred always took off. However, at a certain point in his life in Shepherd Community, Fred exclaimed, "I am ruined! Where can I go after I have begun to experience this kind of community? God won't let me run!"

The support network will stand with you and go to war. They will not bail out when things get rough. Personal agendas will be replaced with Jesus' agenda, and there will be no backing out. They have already been through the rough times and their faith and commitment have kept them in the group. The seventy are willing to "go and die" with you.

The vision has been internalized. Values are owned. Loyalty has been established. The support core is compelled to follow on even in the face of opposition and danger.

The Support Network is About Implementation

The support network is made up of people Thomas Kuhn describes as "men who will develop it to the point where hardheaded arguments can be produced and multiplied." During this stage, the vision is implemented. The infrastructure is established. Lessons are learned. Bugs are worked out. Testing is completed. Materials are developed. Methods are proved. Leaders are identified.

Jesus sent out the disciples as the seventy to learn about His kingdom, His power and how unbelievers would react to them. During this time His support network of seventy learned about evangelism in the world and edification in community life.

Seventy is a good number to learn about implementation. It is large enough to contain several of the basic units of 10's (cells) and large enough to model the other leadership units of 50's and 100's. The mechanics and dynamics of the cell church can be experienced in a group of this size, yet the number is still small enough for the innovative leaders to control, adapt, change and monitor the process. Seventy provides enough people to set a viable model without overwhelming the process with large numbers.

THE SUPPORT NETWORK DIES TO "HIDDEN AGENDAS"

Those who become part of the support network learn to lay down their own hidden agendas in order to be part of a common vision. For the most part, Christians today cluster around causes and tasks rather than around community with Christ. The person with some agenda other than Christ when he comes into a group is thinking "I will relate to you only if the group will accept this assumption or premise. Otherwise, I will not be part of the group." This is a form of control that destroys community. During the forming of the support network of seventy, hidden agendas are exposed and laid down or the journey to becoming a cell church is stopped dead!

Even good *personal* agendas destroy the process of developing prototype community. My agenda may be the spiritual welfare of my children. Your agenda may be in-depth Bible study. Someone else's agenda may be the working of the gifts, or worship, or discipleship or evangelism. Some may champion worthy political causes as their agenda of choice. However, no matter how inherently good an agenda, it still destroys the process of building community, not because it is a *bad* agenda but because it is "my agenda." This is a festering abscess of self-will, just waiting to impose itself as a condition for fellowship upon the group.

Imagine being part of a group trying to move toward a single vision where every person is defending a different set of positions, propositions and agendas. Such personal agendas limit drastically the areas into which the group will journey and restricts the freedom of the Spirit. It fragments the focus of the group, dissipates the spiritual dynamics and ultimately sets one person against every other person in the group if others do not share the personal view or the way of living out that view. My agenda is a subtle attempt to personally control the group's vision rather than to trust Christ to control it. Personal agendas separate a group into enclaves of selfish interest and comfort zones that can't be touched or compromised.

How can we know if the network of seventy is operating around personal agendas rather than around Christ as the agenda? Look for the word "if" in the group, either spoken or lived out in actions. Personal agendas thrive in the atmosphere of conditional relationships. "I will be part of the group *if* you or the group behave in a certain way; *if* you will do a certain thing; *if* you will believe certain doctrines; *if* you act toward me in a certain way; *if* I can exert my influence upon the group!"

Do you understand the devastation wrought by the word *if?* The user is stating that his or her relationship to the community is conditional. Community simply cannot survive in a conditional atmosphere. When we place our requirements upon the group, community is dead. True community has no condition but love.

Dietrich Bonhoeffer was born in Germany in 1906. His career as a theologian, writer, and teacher was rooted in Berlin, his boyhood home. During Hitler's reign, Bonhoeffer spoke out boldly against the Nazi government. In the late 1930's, Bonhoeffer headed a clandestine seminary, where he lived in Christian community with twenty-five vicars. He was imprisoned for his active role in the Resistance Movement and executed at the age of thirty-nine by the German Gestapo on April 5, 1945 at the very end of the war.

During his time in prison, he wrote *The Cost of Discipleship* and *Life Together* on scraps of paper which were smuggled out through sympathetic prison guards. The following reflections on living as the Body of Christ are from the latter work and reveal how seriously Bonhoeffer took conditional commitment in community:

Every human wish dream that is injected into the Christian community is a hindrance to genuine community and must be banished if genuine community is to survive. He who loves his dream of a community more than the Christian community itself

becomes a destroyer of the latter, even though his personal intentions may be ever so honest and earnest and sacrificial . . . The
man who fashions a visionary ideal of community demands that
it be realized by God, by others, and by himself. He enters the
community of Christians with his demands, sets up his own law
and judges the brethren and God Himself accordingly . . . When
things do not go his way he calls the effort a failure. When his
ideal picture is destroyed, he sees the community going to smash.
So he becomes, first an accuser of his brethren, then an accuser
of God, and finally the despairing accuser of himself.[2]

The defining characteristic of the support network is not numbers but
attitudes. It is true a cell church must have at least seventy adults who
have learned how to function as a cell church. Even more important is to
have seventy who, in the process of learning how to be a cell church, have
learned the attitude and mind of Christ and live in commitment and
servanthood.

The support network of seventy committed disciples were among the
120 who moved toward the upper room in Jerusalem where they waited
in prayer, all of one mind and accord. Out of the spirit of the seventy, the
base congregation will be empowered to be Christ's Body. Without a
support network living with Christ and following Him to the upper room,
the base congregation cannot be birthed.

Strategic Phases	Schaller's Change Process	New Testament Numbers	Jesus' Continuum	Vision Action
Preparation	Convergence	Prophetic Word (Jesus)	Cell Church Vision	Conceived
P R O T O T Y P E	Initiating Set	2-3 people	Innovation	Introduced
	Legitimating Sponsorship	12 people	Core Leadership	Owned
	Execution Set	70 people	Support Network	Implemented
Critical Mass / O P E R A T I O N A L	**Fulfillment of Charter**	**120 people**	**Base Congregation**	**Empowered**
		3000-5000	Church Expansion	Expanded

20

JESUS' BASE
CONGREGATION REMNANT

The small group, then, must be both supplemental
and normative—supplemental in that it does not
replace corporate worship; normative in the sense of
being basic church structure,
equally important with corporate worship.
—Howard Snyder

W hen He ascended to heaven, Jesus left one base congregation of 120 in the upper room. Today Christ builds the same kind of church He planted in the first century. When the base congregation finally comes together everything necessary to be the Body of Christ is in place. Christ has not called us to build a church of thousands, but to let Him form His base congregation of 120 around us. Inherent within one base congregation of 120 to 200 *upper room* Christians is the essential infrastructure to be a church of a thousand or tens of thousands. No other structure is required. Simply multiplying the mechanics and dynamics of that congregational unit can result in unlimited growth.

YOIDO TRANSITIONED THROUGH A REMNANT

For years I tried to understand the Yoido Full Gospel Church, the 750,000 member church in Seoul, South Korea. How did this 2400 member traditional church transition into a dynamic, exploding cell church? The secret is right there in Dr. Cho's own writings:

I was only twenty-eight years old, but my body was a wreck. The doctor had told me to give up preaching and choose some other profession. But despite the condition of my body, I felt tremendous excitement. God had spoken to me out of His Word during those days I lay on my bed. He had unveiled a whole plan to me for restructuring our church so that I would not have to carry the ministerial load alone. I was eager to put it into practice, because I was convinced it would work.

However, I could not simply go back to the church and order the members to implement the plan. Our church had 2,400 members, and it had a board of deacons that would have to approve any changes in the structure or the ministry of the church.

"Lord, this is your plan," I prayed. "How can they fail to accept it, since it is your will?" I was confident there would be no opposition.

Dr. Cho realized the importance of involving the decision making body of the church in the vision. For Yoido Full Gospel Church this meant the deacon board. What he found was not open opposition but something just as disturbing.

A month after I was back on my feet, I called the deacon board together and said, "As you know, I am very sick, and I can't carry out all the work of the church, especially counseling and home visitation. And I cannot pray for the sick or even pray with people to be filled with the Holy Spirit."

I told them the things God had revealed to me in Scripture, and I said I was releasing them to carry out the ministry. I told them they needed to stand on their own feet. Then I presented the plan as God had given it to me. I showed the deacons how home cell meetings would work, and I laid out all of the scriptural support I had for this new system.

"Yes, you do have a good biblical argument," one of the deacons said. "This kind of arrangement would seem to be of the Lord. But we have not been trained to do the kinds of things you do. That's why we pay you to be our pastor."

"I am a busy man," said another deacon. "When I return home from work, I'm tired, and I need the privacy of my home. I would not be able to lead a home meeting."

There was not much other comment. Everyone basically agreed that the idea was scripturally sound, but they didn't see how it could work at Full Gospel Central Church. There seemed to be no way I could motivate them. No one got angry; they were simply convinced it couldn't be done.

Dr. Cho was up against a big problem. It became obvious during the meeting the decision making body of the church would not be the group to implement the vision. What could be done? Was the vision doomed?

After a period of prayer and searching the Scriptures, Mrs. Choi and I were discussing the various alternatives to implementing the home cell group plan, and together we hit upon the idea of using the women of the church.
    As we continued to pray for it, while I poured my heart out to the Lord, Mrs. Choi said, "I believe God has revealed this way to us because it is His way. I believe we should call the deaconesses together and present the plan to them."[1]

That was the most critical point in the development of the Yoido Full Gospel Church into a cell church. At that moment, God established a base congregation remnant which would allow it to grow to its present phenomenal size. The call went out and 200 women responded. Notice, this remnant represented almost 10% of the total membership of the church. God providentially gave the necessary remnant to transition that church into His cell church model for the twentieth century. The 200 remnant was the key to transition.
    According to Karen Hurston, who grew up in Yoido Full Gospel Church, this initial group of 200 processed through several cycles before the infrastructure for the remnant was complete. She comments that "with few exceptions, those first groups collapsed."[2] Dr. Cho then gave attention to special problems which had caused the groups to fail and proceeded to strengthen the cell infrastructure.
    It is important for us to see that Yoido Full Gospel Church made the transition from a traditional 2400 member church to a cell church by learning how to do it in a 200 person remnant prototype. And we must not overlook the fact it took them several cell cycles to get the prototype right.

How Do You Eat an Elephant?

In Thailand we used to ask, "How do you eat an elephant?" The answer: "One bite at a time." How do you begin a cell church? One congregation at a time. That's how Jesus did it in the first century, and that is how He does it in the twentieth century.

A stage by stage strategy makes sense from a biblical as well as practical standpoint. Please give careful consideration to the process before you begin a church from scratch or begin to transition a church of any size. The numbers that concern Jesus are not the thousands. Jesus is interested in two or three innovators who grasp His church vision; twelve core leaders, who will leave their nets and follow Him; seventy committed supporters, who will implement the concepts and walk with Him to Jerusalem in the face of death; and finally, one hundred and twenty empowered to be a base remnant. This is Jesus' continuum, introduced in Chapters 15.

Understanding the kind of church Jesus builds is very comforting. One base congregation is possible. I can picture a remnant of 120 and can conceptualize the infrastructure necessary to support one base congregation. A church of thousands is too large and imposing to develop a realistic implementing strategy.

Get this continuum in your mind and then get it into your strategy. This is the leadership template Jesus uses in developing the first base congregation:

Two to three Innovators begin the process.
A Leadership Core of 12 is gathered.
The Support Network of 70 followers sets the Prototype.
A Base Congregation of at least 120 adults births multiplication.

Base Congregation Characteristics

What will a base congregation with the potential of exponential multiplication look like?

1. There will be 12 to 15 healthy cells living together in New Testament community. The key word here is healthy cells. Some dysfunctional cells may also be in the mix, but at least 12 to 15 healthy functional cells are necessary to be a base congregation.

2. All necessary leaders are being produced from cell life. Interns are in place for every level of leader, and interns are being systematically

trained and developed. Volunteer supervisors of three to five cells are overseeing the cell leaders of 10's and coordinating the work of the ministry at the most basic cell level. Pastors of 100's are casting the vision and giving general direction to the church.

3. Balanced celebration worship flows out of cell life and supports life in cells as the basic church activity.

4. Unbelievers are contacted and cultivated through cell life in natural *oikos* relationship evangelism. Cells are also reaching the lost through special contact groups that meet the unbelievers at their felt needs. Seekers are also being absorbed into the cells. The church is not dependent upon the large group meeting for growth but grows from cell life.

5. New members are developed into mature disciples through a systematic equipping track.

6. A strong prayer base undergirds all activities of the church in personal prayer, prayer in cells and prayer in leadership meetings and in large corporate meetings. The remnant is expectantly waiting upon God to supply His power for dynamic exponential multiplication. A church that reaches this point might want to set aside a month of prayer, fasting and waiting on the Lord in order to acknowledge that only God can empower a church so that exponential multiplication can happen as in the early church.

TRANSITION STRATEGY

God transitioned Yoido Full Gospel Church and some of the more recent successful cell church transitions through a remnant transition strategy. However, the temptation of most pastors who want to become a cell church is to try to transition the entire church at one time. This is almost impossible to do for several reasons:

- *What do you do with all of the existing activities and programs while the transition process is taking place?*
- *How are church vision and values changed in the broader church body without a working model?*
- *How is cell life experienced and the necessary infrastructure set up in the church overnight?*
- *How are church leaders released to develop the prototype at the same time they are responsible for the existing structure?*

A leader must think *remnant*. With a small and manageable number of the total church members, a cell church Prototype can be established through which the church can transition into a cell church. The chart in Figure 10 explains this remnant transition process. Each circle represents an aspect of the transition process. The two circles at the top, called remnant transition and values transition, occur simultaneously. The bottom circle, called structure transition, grows out of the other two circles and will only be effectively accomplished if the remnant and values transitions are successful.

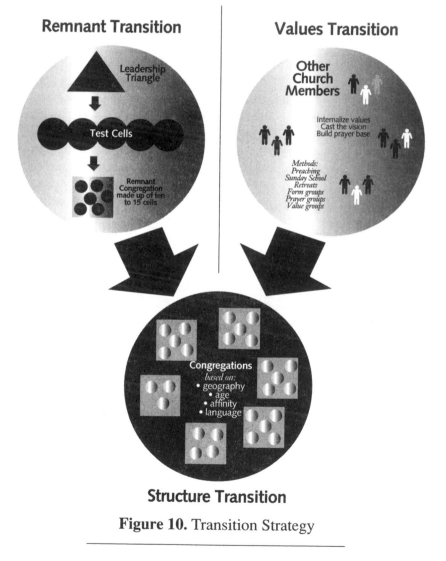

Figure 10. Transition Strategy

UNDERSTANDING THE REMNANT TRANSITION CIRCLE

The transitioning process moves along Jesus' leadership continuum of two to three innovators, twelve core leaders, seventy in the support network and finally one hundred and twenty waiting on the Lord for empowerment (figure 10, the top left circle).

If a church could set aside in the very beginning at least 10% of its active membership to discover how to be a cell church, the process would be greatly accelerated. However, most churches will become a remnant only through a more deliberate stage by stage process. The initial remnant will be small in the beginning and then grow as it moves through Jesus' leadership continuum.

The continuum is a blessing because it allows a model to be set without demanding that everyone in the church understand or participate in it. It leaves the existing structure in place until alternate structures have been discovered and tested out. This remnant approach allows time to bring the members along slowly. It does not demand that everyone understand and commit to the total vision immediately.

To build the remnant, the church will process through the continuum discussed in Chapter 18. Begin with the first leadership discovery cell. Then those from the initial cell will lead the secondary leadership discovery cells. After these first two cycles, more people will be brought into the test cell cycles from the main congregation. The remnant will process through several test cell cycles, increasing until there are 12-15 cells. This time is when the prototype, discussed in Chapters 16 and 17, is being developed. It is the time to:

1. Discover the mechanics and dynamics of basic Christian community.
2. Establish 12 to 15 healthy cells through several test cycles of six to nine months each.
3. Insert essential components into the cell infrastructure, such as the Jethro leadership structure, an equipping track, intern training, celebration worship, prayer and overflow evangelism.

The principles of the continuum are applied to the transition of a large church just like they are to a new church plant. The difference lies in the fact that the transitioning church has a ready base of people to insert into the test cells.

UNDERSTANDING THE VALUES TRANSITION CIRCLE

While the prototype is being established within the selected remnant, important elements are being introduced into the broader church body. The senior pastor and senior leaders are the primary change agents for the rest of the church, as well (figure 10, the top right circle).

The vision of New Testament cell life is cast in the entire church body. Specific details of the vision are given to the whole membership but only to the degree the leadership of the church buys into the vision and values. There is no need to dump on the whole congregation every detail about what it means to be a cell church until the leadership groups within the church are committed to the vision and are actually implementing it as part of the remnant. Detailed discussions of specific structures that will be streamlined or phased out are counterproductive. Structural changes should only be discussed in detail with the entire church body after a broad base of leaders support that action and the value base for changing that structure has been internalized and accepted by the leaders and people.

Values in the whole congregation are internalized through sermons and special studies taught within their present structure—Sunday school, Sunday worship, prayer meetings, etc. *Remember, you must never change a structure until you have changed the corresponding values.* When values are actually changed some structures can be streamlined or eliminated. Suppress the inner compulsion to explain the vision in terms of structures that must be changed. Instead explain the vision in terms of values that must be lived out.

Pre-cells in the broader membership will help prepare the whole church for transition. These groups are not cell groups, leadership discovery cells, or even test cells. They might be prayer groups or groups studying New Testament values such as community, evangelism, or how to equip the saints. Such groups involve the broader church body in the transition process, teach group communication skills and help church members understand the process of change. Pre-cells also provide a way to prepare selected members to move over into cell life when additional cells are organized during the test cell cycles.

People will not want to change unless their values have first changed and then only if they are able to see an alternate working model of what they are adopting. This is why it is so important to develop the prototype through the remnant while the whole congregation is being prepared for cell life.

UNDERSTANDING THE RESTRUCTURING CIRCLE

After an existing church has developed its remnant base congregation, it needs to divide its members into working congregational units of 60 to 200 adults. Organizing the church into units of 100's will provide a way for the church to make the final transition into a cell church. Within each of these congregations, plant some of those from the remnant group to be leaders, interns and core members of the new cells (figure 10, the bottom circle).

Just before rice planting season in the Central Plains of Thailand, unusual plots can be seen from the highway. These plots look like lush green carpets of grass, like putting greens on a golf course. They are in fact seed beds for the rice that will soon be planted in the rice patties.

When the fields are flooded and the time for planting arrives, these seed beds are carefully pulled up and tied into small bundles. These bundles are taken to one of the larger paddies. Each separate rice plant is planted by hand. One small seed bed contains enough rice plants to cover an area hundreds of times the size of the original seed bed.

This is a picture of the remnant strategy in a church. The remnant prototype that is being carefully planted and grown over the months is at the proper time seeded out into the paddies, the congregations of 100. From one small remnant, the whole church can be planted with cell church concepts and structures. Eventually all of the church will look just like the original remnant seed bed, green and lush.

CONGREGATIONS: "LEAN, MEAN, WORKING MACHINES"

In the cell church context, congregation (units of 100) refers to a special kind of organizational unit within the cell church, often referred to as a *Zone* of cells. A congregation consists of a group of 10 to 25 cells (basic Christian communities) that network together. The congregation is a working spiritual unit that helps enable cell leaders and cells to do the work of ministry. A pastor over 100's coordinates the work in a geographical or people strata of the church. The congregation in a pure cell church is a "lean, mean working machine" focused upon releasing the dynamic life of the basic cell units. It minimizes administration and maximizes ministry at the cell level. Networking of the 100's focuses on the small groups of 10's where every task of the church comes alive in dynamic cell life.

Congregations provide a framework so that needs can be cared for at the cell level. When a transitioning church is restructured into cell church congregations, every member becomes part of a congregation and begins to draw their ministry from the cells (units of 10), rather than the pastoral staff.

In forming up these congregations you might have the following considerations:

- Geography will generally be a major factor. Cell churches need a geographic grid.
- Cultural/ethnic makeup of the 100's
- Age groupings such as youth or senior citizens
- Socio-economic factors
- Language groupings
- Special needs such as ministry to the deaf

Fit and Retrofit

The base congregation remnant must be established in an existing church or a new church start if either is to become an operational cell church. The only difference between a new church plant and a transitioning church is that the base congregation principles and infrastructure must be retrofitted into the existing structures of the transitioning church.

Fit the remnant together in a new church start. This means the stages must be built from scratch since no structure exists. *Retrofit* a cell church remnant into an existing church structure. This means the stages must be remodeled back into the existing structure, molding and shaping what is already in place into a cell model.

Scores of existing churches, some with thousands of members, are proceeding along Jesus' three and a half year continuum. Remnant base congregations of 120 to 200 adults are being carefully formed with existing members. As these churches complete the continuum, we can compare the rate of their growth and the strength of their infrastructure with other churches which have ignored the stage by stage process and have attempted to go directly to operational cells. However, the trend is already evident: large churches which first develop a remnant base congregation move more quickly into total cell life than churches that ignore the remnant process.

Strategic Phases	Schaller's Change Process	New Testament Numbers	Jesus' Continuum	Vision Action
Preparation	Convergence	Prophetic Word (Jesus)	Cell Church Vision	Conceived
P R O T O T Y P E	Initiating Set	2-3 people	Innovation	Introduced
	Legitimating Sponsorship	12 people	Core Leadership	Owned
	Execution Set	70 people	Support Network	Implemented
Critical Mass / O P E R A T I O N A L	Fulfillment of Charter	120 people	Base Congregation	Empowered
		3000-5000	Church Expansion	Expanded

21

JESUS' CRITICAL MASS

*Much of the uniqueness of Christianity, in its origi-
nal emergence, consisted of the fact that simple
people could be amazingly powerful when they were
members one of another.*
—Elton Trueblood

P icture this—it is fifty days after the Passover in the year 30 AD,
seven weeks after the death and resurrection of Christ, and ten
days after His ascension to heaven. You are one of the 120 followers in the upper room in Jerusalem. The surviving eleven disciples are
there along with the women, the family of Jesus, and others who followed
during those action packed three and a half years.

During the season of Pentecost, the Jews celebrate the grain harvest
and the giving of the law at Mount Sinai. For ten days after the ascension,
persevering prayer with one heart and mind has consumed you, along
with the rest in the Upper Room. The group, as John Stott commented, is
"poised ready to fulfill Christ's command just as soon as he has fulfilled
his promise."[1] The last thing Jesus commanded was to wait and the Spirit
would come (Luke 24:49, Acts 1:8).

The air crackles with electricity, and the silence is deafening. Expectancy
is heavy in the room. Everyone present senses something incredible is about
to happen. Jesus Christ is expected to be in your midst, as He promised. Stott
said, "Though the place left vacant by Judas has been filled by Matthias, the
place left vacant by Jesus has not yet been filled by the Spirit."[2] You are waiting for the King to return, for the owner to take possession.

You have witnessed the resurrection power that raised Him from the dead and took Him up into Heaven. You now know nothing is impossible with Christ. Then it happens! The sound of rushing wind and tongues of fire fall upon you. You experience God in His Spirit with your whole being.

WHAT IS HAPPENING HERE?

Critical mass is "the minimum amount of fissionable material capable of producing a self-sustaining chain reaction."[3] At Pentecost, Christ began incarnating Himself into the church through the Spirit. The upper room has become the spiritual epicenter of the living presence, the mighty power and divine purpose of God on earth. What the stable was to the physical incarnation of Christ in the world in flesh, the upper room has become to the spiritual incarnation of Christ in the world through His church. The Shekinah of God which accompanied the children of Israel in the wilderness, was in the midst of the camp in the tabernacle, and departed the temple Holy of Holies at the death of Jesus *has returned!* The incarnation seed sown by Christ in His death on the cross has been born at Pentecost. Critical mass has been reached in that upper room.

JESUS ALWAYS BUILDS A CRITICAL MASS

From the account in Acts, one might think a spiritual time bomb was waiting to be detonated. The one hundred and twenty disciples were an explosive critical mass because they had the necessary components to be a self-sustaining chain reaction. What they had experienced, how Jesus prepared them, their relationship with Him before and after His resurrection, the evidence of His resurrection power, and the indwelling Spirit built up to an explosive point. "The Spirit is known henceforward as God's gracious power and equally as the presence of Christ himself,"[4] Stott said.

The 120 in the upper room were a critical mass because the presence of Christ came upon them, followed by His power, which resulted in His purpose as they streamed out into the streets to witness of Christ. The Church continues to be birthed in the same way today.

I am not suggesting the same unusual events must be duplicated when Jesus builds His Church today. It is not the spectacular events but the spiritual incarnation that is necessary for the Church to be birthed in the first century or the twentieth century. God's indwelling, abiding, incarnate and living presence within His earthly spiritual Body, the Church, is essential for the Church to be born, otherwise the church is only a human organization. Jess Moody told us, "If our only success 'is that which can be explained in terms of organization and management—that is, something the world could do with the same expenditure of effort and technique, the world will one day finally repudiate us.'"[5]

In one sense, Pentecost is a one time event as with the incarnation. However, this event continues to flow across history. Christ, born one time at Bethlehem, is also born in my life. The Spirit comes at Pentecost as a one time event, but that event continues in my life. The Church is empowered at Pentecost, but that same empowering must happen in every church. The incarnation, cross, resurrection and Pentecost events continue to be lived out in my life and the life of the church.

Something of the power and life of the first Pentecost accompanies the church whenever He indwells it. Bernard J. Lee and Michael A. Cowan point out this remarkable expectation in their book *Dangerous Memories:*

> Christians who over the centuries have prayed for the gift of Spirit that enkindles fires in our hearts, and remakes the face of the earth, are not surprised that One who invented church on Pentecost can re-invent it whenever it is timely. History suggests that Pentecost is a moveable feast.[6]

No "Critical Mass" Without Incarnation

What does "Christ indwelling His Church" mean? We use these words to explain the unique relationship of Christ with the church. That relationship is one of continuing incarnation. Only this living presence of Christ in His Church can account for the church becoming an explosive critical mass.

Ray Stedman identifies the holy mystery of the church as the incarnation. God lives in his people, in His Church. That is the secret of the Church.

> The secret of the church is that Christ lives in it and the message of the church to the world is to declare him, to talk about Jesus Christ. . . . There [Eph. 2:19-22] is the holy mystery of the

church—it is the dwelling place of God. He lives in his people.
That is the great calling of the church—to make visible the invisible Christ.[7]

Stedman understood the importance of the incarnation to the doctrine
of the church. He believed what happened on a small scale in the first
century continues today on a large scale through the Church:

> We shall make a great mistake if we think incarnation ended with
> the earthly life of Jesus. The incarnation is still going on. The life
> of Jesus is still being manifest among men, but now no longer
> through an individual physical body, limited to one place on
> earth, but through a complex, corporate body called the church.
>   In his second account (the book of Acts) Dr. Luke continues
> the record of Jesus at work among mankind, but this time through
> his new body, the church. The church, therefore, when it lives in
> and by the Spirit, is to be nothing more nor less than the exten-
> sion of the life of Jesus to the whole world in any age.[8]

Baptist missiologist and New Testament scholar, William O. Carver,
draws some astounding conclusions about the meaning of the incarnation
to the church today. He believed in the "continuing incarnation of Christ
in the world" and that the Church is the "growing Body" of Christ. "The
church is the extension of his (Christ's) incarnation. A local church is the
manifestation of Christ in its community."[9]
    In Ephesians, Carver found the Church "so intimately and so essen-
tially related to the Christ and to his meaning in history as to constitute
his growing self-realization in the process of accomplishing the ends of
his incarnation. The Church is his growing Body, that in it He is Himself
growing into maturity."[10]

COMMUNITY INCARNATION

God manifests Himself into the world within His Church in at least
two ways. Scripture indicates He manifested Himself in the world as a
Person (Christ) and God manifests Himself in the world in community
(Church). In both cases, God uses the most basic stuff of life as the means
of His manifestation. When He physically manifested Himself (the incarnation) into the world in Christ, He used physical cells. The meaning of

the incarnation is unique because it teaches God was in the world in our kind of form, our kind of body completely vulnerable to our hurts, pains, sins, temptations and sufferings. His physical body was formed out of biological cells, just like our own body.

God also continues to incarnate Himself into the world in a second way, in the church. God is now spiritually incarnated in a community context. Paul suggests this in Ephesians 2:21-22: "In whom (Christ) you also are being built together (this is not a personal or individual event but a corporate one) into a dwelling of God in the Spirit." The church is the dwelling of God. That is, spiritual incarnation takes place in and through the ecclesia (church).

The incarnation of Christ into the world in a physical context has been part of my belief system since I was a child. However, the incarnation of Christ in His spiritual community context has taken years to crystallize in my life.

This community incarnation concept boggles the mind. Through the Holy Spirit, God once again incarnates Himself into a cell context, but this time not a biological cell but a sociological cell through which He becomes community. He once again uses the basic stuff of life to form His spiritual Body operating on earth. The same cell context God used to express Himself in physical life (biological cells) He uses to express Himself in community life (social cell units).

Ray Stedman understood the unique concept of the "continuing incarnation" of Christ in and through His Church.

Jesus Christ is not off in some remote corner of the universe (heaven), nor has he left his people here to struggle on and do the best they can until he comes back again. This was never the divine intent nor is it the New Testament pattern. Christ is alive and has been at work in human society for twenty centuries, just as he said he would be: *Lo I am with you always, to the close of the age* (Matt. 28:20).[11]

Biblical scholar C. H. Dodd considered the church to be unique because of its relationship to Christ:

. . . after "forty days" . . . Christ finally vanished from human view: "a cloud removed him from their sight." *That* chapter is closed, never to be repeated. But the entire New Testament is witness that the real presence of Christ was not withdrawn when the "appearances" ceased. The unique and evanescent meetings with the risen Lord triggered off a new kind of relation which proved permanent. . . . In the fellowship the presence of the Lord no longer meant a sudden flash of recognition, utterly convincing but soon over. It was an enduring reality, creative of a new corporate life.

Within that corporate life, as it matured and expanded, and larger perspectives broadened out, their understanding of what had happened went deeper. It was not simply that their lost Leader had come back to them. God himself had come to them in a way altogether new. And that put the whole story in a fresh light.[12]

No critical mass exists without the special indwelling of Christ in His Church. Our administration, motivation and promotion will not produce a critical mass. Such human endeavors can produce a good organization but without the incarnation of Christ the church will never explode in New Testament power.

JUMP START

After critical mass is reached, a cell church can begin to jump start new work. Establishing the first prototype is painful. Every step must be carefully learned, implemented and tested. However, once a church begins its exponential multiplication growth, it does not have to go back to the start every time it plants a new church.

An operational cell church can jump start new work by sending out a prepared remnant to be the nucleus of a new start. This nucleus could be twelve, seventy or even one hundred and twenty. The larger the initial remnant, the faster the new work will be established and itself reach critical mass. Yoido Full Gospel church has sent out large congregations to form new churches. More than 500,000 members are part of churches formed out of the mother church of 750,000.

This approach to church planting will revolutionize the way missions has been done for the past century. We have had what I call a "margarine strategy" of missions which is to spread missionaries just as thin and as far as possible. Mission sending agencies typically assign a couple by themselves to begin work in some geographical area, often off the beaten path. Few teams are sent out, since planting churches out from strong base congregations has never caught on as a strategy.

Jump starting from base cell churches will greatly increase the potential for exponential growth. Such a ready-made remnant will already understand what it means to be be a part of a cell church and will have enough people to immediately model cell life, cell leadership and evangelism. Jump starting such critical masses all over the world can be as explosive as it was in the first century, when the *diaspora* scattered the Jerusalem believers across the Roman Empire.

22

JESUS' CRITICAL MASS COMPONENTS

Give me 100 men who hate nothing but sin
and love God with all their hearts and
I will shake the world for Christ!
—John Wesley

C ritical mass does not just automatically happen. Certain components must come together in a prescribed way to cause a chain
reaction. A component serves as one of the parts of a whole. If those
components are missing from the mix, the whole will be incomplete and
critical mass will not be reached. A bomb without the right electronic
system, the right chemicals, placed in the right casing, is no bomb at all. The
business world recognizes the importance of this critical mass phenomenon:

> To get any idea rolling, you need to build enthusiasm. When the
> idea is supported by a sufficient number of diverse people, it reaches
> a "critical mass." It takes off under its own steam, giving the
> impression of a growing, formidable movement and a sense of
> momentum. The size of the critical mass can vary from just a few
> key people to the whole company. In the early stages of change, the
> critical mass builds as key opinion leaders shift from a neutral to
> supportive position, or at least from resistance to indecision.[1]

What components made up Jesus' critical mass? What is necessary to
achieve the kind of explosion described in Acts of the Apostles?

NUMERICAL COMPONENT

Sufficient numbers are required to allow a chain reaction. A certain number of people committed to change must be gathered to move the change process along. An existing church will gather these people from existing members. A new start must gather them from among unbelievers, prodigal Christians or Christians sent by God. A sufficient number of people, when joined together in a common purpose, can cause synergistic results far beyond their numbers. Evidently, Jesus determined one hundred and twenty adults was sufficient to fulfill His vision.

Remember John Wesley's quote: "Give me one hundred men who hate nothing but sin and love God with all their hearts, and I will shake the world for Christ!" Wesley recognized the power of a sufficient number joined together in a common passionate cause.

The number 120 is not magical. If you are in a smaller church, your critical mass may be less than one hundred and twenty people. However, you will need a significant percentage of your church body to form the critical mass. If you are a much larger church of hundreds or thousands, the good news is that one hundred and twenty members is sufficient to ultimately transition the entire church.

Peter Wagner recognizes the importance of the critical mass in his book *Church Planting for a Greater Harvest:*

> In nuclear physics the critical mass is the minimum amount of fissionable material necessary to produce a chain reaction. In church planting it indicates the size a viable nucleus needs to be at the time of going public, if the church is to grow well.
>
> If the long-range plan for the church is to be under 200, the critical mass can be as small as 25 or 30 adults. However, if the plan is for the church to grow to over 200 that is too small. The critical mass should be between 50 and 100 adults.[2]

VISION COMPONENT

A cell church vision is a necessary component for driving a group of people toward critical mass. George Barna, in his book *The Power of Vision*, describes vision in a series of graphic images. For Barna vision is:

A peek at the future that God has intended for each disciple
A dream with wheels and a road map
A focus among the overwhelming amount of needs
A God-sized idea
Seeing the invisible and making it visible
Sanctified dreams[3]

Vision is an essential component for reaching critical mass. I am not referring to a vision statement posted around the church. Vision in a kingdom sense means passion, calling, a compulsion from God, an oughtness. This kind of vision is not something I catch but something that catches me. I do not act upon this vision, it acts upon me. Helen Keller was asked, "What would be worse than being born blind?" She replied, "To have sight without vision."

Oswald Chambers, in *My Utmost for His Highest*, describes vision as a process being worked out in our lives. "God gives us the vision, then He takes us down to the valley to alter us into the shape of the vision, and it is in the valley that so many of us faint and give way. Every vision will be made real if we will have patience."

A vision is something working on our lives, not something we are working on. Chambers again speaks of vision: "We cannot attain to a vision, we must live in the inspiration of it until it accomplishes itself."[4]

Barna also recognized this "altering" aspect to vision. "In suggesting that vision deals with that which is preferable, we are insinuating that vision entails change. Vision is never about maintaining the status quo. Vision is about stretching reality to extend beyond the existing stage."[5]

In the Upper Room, we see a group of people who had been altered into the shape of the vision Christ had brought from the Father. They had passed through the valley and were now formed into a dynamic unit: the Body of Christ, a critical mass. Every person in the Bible used to fulfill God's vision experienced this altering process down in the valley. They did not do the vision but were altered by the vision so God could do it though them. Abraham was altered into God's vision. Then God fulfilled the vision through him. So were Moses and David. Look at the altering process in Peter and Paul. They both experienced the valley before God could use them to implement His vision.

Our approach to vision is, "Here is God's vision, now let me get busy doing it." That is why we must be altered before we can live out God's vision. When we are altered into God's vision we then say, "Here is God's vision, now let me see how God is going to shape me into His vision."

A church leader near Washington, D.C. received this word from God about vision, "Where the vision is unclear, the cost is always too high." That is why we must clearly see God's vision. The life of community and ministry that Jesus has for us is so important we must count the cost as Jesus suggested. If the vision is not clear, somewhere down the road we will bail out.

COMMITMENT COMPONENT

Without absolute commitment to Christ, no critical mass will occur. Over and over again, Jesus sought to test and strengthen the commitment of His followers. "Who do men say that I am?" "Foxes have holes and the birds of the air nests but the Son of Man has no where to lay His head." "Will you also turn away?" Critical mass will only come out of intense and unconditional commitment. We do not arrive at this kind of commitment overnight. Commitment is learned out on the cutting edge in cell life, the same place Jesus honed the commitment of His followers. Commitment is developed within the crucible of cell life. Their commitment is tested by doing the vision. Living together in cell life develops the kind of commitment necessary to reach critical mass.

Jesus has the same standards for commitment for every generation of those who would follow him.

> If anyone wishes to come after Me, let him deny himself, and take up his cross daily, and follow Me. For whoever wishes to save his life shall lose it, but whoever loses his life for My sake, he is the one who will save it. For what is a man profited if he gains the whole world, and loses or forfeits himself? For whoever is ashamed of Me and My words, of him will the Son of Man be ashamed when He comes in His glory, and the glory of the Father and of the holy angels (Luke 9:23-26).

Community reveals and unveils this kind of commitment. Elton Trueblood challenged us by saying:

> We shall not be saved by anything less than commitment, and the commitment will not be effective unless it finds expression in a

committed fellowship. If we have any knowledge of human nature, we begin by rejecting the arrogance of self-sufficiency. Committed men need the fellowship not because they are strong, but because they are—and know that they are—fundamentally sinful and weak.[6]

Following Christ in His community requires a commitment measured by death. This is what Jesus taught His disciples before they arrived at the upper room. The upper room was about His death but also about their own death to their agendas, their pride, their dreams of personal glory and position and their earthly comforts and rewards. Only this kind of commitment will reach critical mass.

VALUES COMPONENT

Values are a thing or quality having intrinsic worth; beliefs or standards. Values are the underlying and deeply held beliefs that influence our actions. What are the values that undergirded Jesus' life? What were the qualities that had intrinsic worth and importance to Jesus? These values are essential to becoming critical mass.

Jesus daily taught His disciples about spiritual values. He did not care if they could recite a creed about the values of the kingdom, but that these values would be internalized in their hearts and lived out in their lives in community. Some of the values He constantly taught were faith, abiding in His indwelling presence, community, ministry, gifts, servanthood, unity, prayer, edification and evangelism. These values form the base from which critical mass intrinsically happens. It is not so much what I value, but what God values. Such values flowing out of the heart of God result in critical mass.

TIME COMPONENT

How many other times had the disciples been together in that same upper room? Probably several. Yet nothing happened like Pentecost because the "fullness of time" had not yet come. Time is required to assemble the mechanics of Jesus' system, but to internalize the dynamics requires even more time. We may understand the working of the cell church rather quickly, but the living of it takes even longer.

Unfortunately, few of us value patience, and as Shakespeare said, "How poor are they that have not patience."[7] Nowhere is this more evident than with church leaders. We want instant gratification and success. Our culture is geared toward a quick fix and a quick buy for everything. Commercials on television make everything seem so easy. It's easy to buy a car, build a house, take off fifty pounds, become a successful businessman, become a millionaire or—grow a big church.

Our impatience with implementing any vision in our church finds it's root in our pride. We always overestimate our ability to make spiritual things happen quickly. Our need for quick fixes and instant success also reveals a basic flaw in our thinking about the church. Many believe that if they apply effort and expertise to the church, it can quickly become successful. This is only true if the church is just an organization we market and administer.

However, time is required for God to build His kind of church. God does everything in the fullness of time. This fullness will not arrive until Jesus prepares a people to be His Church. Much of that time must be given for leaders to learn how to let God do it instead of doing it themselves.

PROCESS COMPONENT

Critical mass is achieved one step at a time through a process. The process for critical mass in the cell church is for the church to develop innovative core leaders, draw together a committed and trained support network and then develop a base congregation infrastructure. To jump over any of this essential process will result in a cell church dud rather than a cell church explosion.

Each stage contains the seeds of the next stage. More followers will be present at each stage than the number necessary for that stage. For instance, by the time there is a leadership core of twelve, more than twelve should be actively participating. You may have 100 followers but still be discipling the twelve core leaders and still learning how to implement with the support network of seventy. However, by the time critical mass is reached, each of the stages must be represented. Innovators, core leaders and a support network form the infrastructure of the developing church. Only then can God's spirit move through these essential stages to create critical mass.

LEADERSHIP COMPONENT

Jesus had a leadership strategy, not a membership strategy. He focused His time and energies on developing leaders and establishing them into a working unit. The cell church will never reach critical mass until leaders have been trained to understand Jesus' cell church system and are committed to implementing it. The old way the church has done leadership through professionals will not facilitate critical mass. The Jethro leadership structure (Exodus 18) must be in place so that Christ has a chain of support and coordination for the 10's, 50's, 100's and 1,000's.

Critical mass will only develop out of submissive, servant leaders. In *A Tale of Three Kings*, Gene Edwards pictures this kind of submission in King David. The following is an allegorical conversation between a young army officer and the last "Mighty Warrior" of King David. The "Mighty Warrior" explains what made David a great leader:

> David showed me submission, not authority. He taught me, not the quick cures of rules and laws, but the art of patience. That is what changed my life. Legalism is nothing but a leader's way of avoiding suffering.
>
> Rules were invented by elders, so they could get to bed early! Men who harp on authority only prove they have none. And kings who make speeches about submission only betray twin fears in their heart—They are not certain they are really true leaders, sent of God. And they live in mortal fear of a rebellion.
>
> My king spoke not of submitting to him. He feared no rebellion . . . because he did not mind if he was dethroned!
>
> David taught me losing, not winning. Giving, not taking. He showed me that the leader, not the follower, is inconvenienced. He shielded us from suffering; he did not mete it out.
>
> He taught me that authority yields to rebellion especially when that rebellion is nothing more dangerous than immaturity, or perhaps stupidity.
>
> . . . authority from God is not afraid of challengers, makes no defense, and cares not one whit if it must be dethroned.[8]

Leadership know how, pride and power do not result in spiritual explosion. Incredibly, only submission and a servant heart can supply the leadership quality to cause Christ's critical mass.

STRUCTURE COMPONENT

The cell church operates with its own unique structures and will not work with the old one-day-a-week church structures. Critical mass will not be reached until cell church structures have been put into place. The primary structure is the cell itself with all other activities and tasks functioning in support of the primary cell structure. Essential structures include a leadership structure, equipping structure, evangelism structure, celebration structure and prayer structure as described in chapters 18 and 20.

Writing about renewal, Howard Snyder, in *Signs of the Spirit,* explains that one dimension of renewal:

> has to do with forms and structures. It is the dimension of renewal concerned with the way we, as believers, live out our lives together. It is the question of the best wineskins for the new wine.
>
> Renewal often dies prematurely for lack of effective structures. The new wine flows through the cracks of our own forms and is soon lost. Renewal becomes a fond memory, not a new way of life.[9]

PRAYER COMPONENT

Prayer is the breath and life of a cell church. Jesus said, "I will build my church . . ." Our part in Christ building His church takes place through prayer and communication with the Master Builder. Because the cell church will not work without Christ building it, the cell church depends totally upon prayer.

How will you be a part of what He is building if you do not hear His heart and His desires? How will leaders know how to minister unless they are in tune with God and empowered by Him? Waiting on Him, not good activity is the key to reaching critical mass.

If your church is not a praying church, one that longs for the presence of God, both personally and corporately, then entering into cells will prove the most frustrating endeavor you have ever tried. One thing is true: if God desires your church to become a cell church, either on this side of implementation or on the other, you will learn to pray. Prayer will become a cry of desperation to the only one who can lead the church through what He desires it to be. Coleman said:

> . . . He emphasized the life of prayer again and again when talking with His disciples, continually enlarging upon its meaning

and application as they were able to comprehend deeper realities of His Spirit. It was an indispensable part of their training, which in turn they would have to transmit to others. One thing is certain. Unless they grasped the meaning of prayer, and learned how to practice it with consistency, not much would ever come from their lives.[10]

Prayer must take on a comprehensive meaning. It must happen at all levels of the church—in the cell meetings, in leadership meetings, in weekly body life of the cells, in the whole church, in families, as individuals. The largest churches in the world do not just have a cell system where everyone can have community life, they are also known for their prayer.

POWER COMPONENT

All the components above can be in place and the whole thing may just sit there. Extraordinary power is required to cause an earthly church composed of physical components such as people, methods and structures to become a spiritual critical mass.

God can supply this component. That is why Jesus commanded the disciples after those three and a half years of preparation to wait in Jerusalem until they had received the "promise." He promised He would return in the Spirit, and they would become His spiritual Body on earth. The promised Spirit is the trigger that activates all of the ingredients and causes the chain reaction of spiritual power to explode.

Critical mass happened at Pentecost, an explosion of spiritual life and community that shook the world. But that explosion was made up of the proper components that Jesus carefully assembled over more than three years which are one hundred and twenty, vision, commitment, values, time, process, leadership, structure, prayer and power. We must give attention to the same components today. Without them the incarnation explosion will not be possible; and we will find ourselves with a critical mess, not a critical mass.

Strategic Phases	Schaller's Change Process	New Testament Numbers	Jesus' Continuum	Vision Action
Preparation	Convergence	Prophetic Word (Jesus)	Cell Church Vision	Conceived
PROTOTYPE	Initiating Set	2-3 people	Innovation	Introduced
	Legitimating Sponsorship	12 people	Core Leadership	Owned
	Execution Set	70 people	Support Network	Implemented
Critical Mass / *OPERATIONAL*	Fulfillment of Charter	120 people	Base Congregation	Empowered
		3000-5000	**Church Expansion**	**Expanded**

CONCLUSION
THE DOCTRINE OF REVOLUTION

It is the depravity of institutions and movements that given in the beginning to express life they often end in throttling that very life. Therefore they need constant review, perpetual criticism, a continuous bringing back to original purposes and spirit. The Christian church is no exception. It is the chief illustration of the above.
—E. Stanley Jones

A s we enter the twenty-first century, many prophetic voices suggest the church must change dramatically and even radically if it is to be God's effective instrument. According to Francis Schaeffer in *Death in the City*, we live in a "post-Christian" world. He makes the following proposition in light of our situation:

> The church in our generation needs reformation, revival and constructive revolution. At times men think of the two words "reformation" and "revival" as standing in contrast one to the other. But this is a mistake. Both words are related to the word "restore."
>
> Reformation refers to a restoration to pure doctrine; revival refers to a restoration in the Christian's life. Reformation speaks of a return to the teachings of Scripture; revival speaks of a life brought into its proper relationship to the Holy Spirit.[1]

In discussing the state of the church, Schaeffer links together four important words—reformation, revival, restoration, and revolution. He concludes that before spiritual revolution of society can happen there must be reformation of doctrine and revival of believers. He suggests here (and spells it out in other writings) a restoration of structure is essential. Resistance is also somewhere there in the mix as well.

Spiritual revolution that will dramatically change the very root of society as we know it follows an equation:

Reformation of Doctrine
  + Revival of God's Spirit
    + Remnant of God's Committed
      + Restoration of the New Testament Design
        = *Spiritual Revolution*

REFORMATION OF DOCTRINE

Reformation of several important doctrines took place more than 500 years ago. Damage previously inflicted upon the doctrine of salvation, authority of Scripture, priesthood of the believer and others was reversed and set on a more biblical path. Of course this is a constant vigil of rethinking the meaning of these doctrines in every age. However, the Reformation did establish a *doctrinal framework* which was missing during the previous 1000 years. Today, it is not necessary for the church to go back through the painful process of reforming the major theological framework of Christianity. That has already been done.

The Reformation has been considered by many as the high point in church history. Since coming into the stream of the cell church, I find myself viewing the Reformation in a different way. What if the Reformation of 500 years ago was preparation for what God is getting ready to do today? What if in God's timetable the reformation of doctrine was only one of the elements in preparing the world for a revolutionary harvest He is preparing for today? Radical? Yes! But when we see events in history as an ongoing process that God prepares for the next events, it is not out of reason. God looks at history in the long run. The events of the Old and New Testament were woven into each other over more than a 2000 year span of history. Isn't modern history important enough to God to warrant this same divine attention?

REVIVAL OF GOD'S SPIRIT

Spiritual revolution begins with reformation of doctrine and moves with the revival of God's Spirit. I am not just talking about "revivalism" although this and the revival of God's Spirit are closely related. We have had periodic times when the church, especially in modern history, has been revived. Such revivals may have energized and reshaped their societies for brief periods, but they have not had long term, lasting effect.

The only hope is for constructive spiritual revolution. This requires a revival of God's Spirit which is the root cause of revivals. In this century God, seems to have poured out His Holy Spirit in special ways. This has not been a matter of discovering a new doctrine of the Holy Spirit. It is at the point of experience and application of the Spirit that revival has taken place.

While orthodox evangelical churches were debating and teaching about the Holy Spirit, there was a movement of God's Spirit into the life of other groups. We have witnessed in the twentieth century the application of the work of the Spirit in many lives. This movement of God's Spirit is among groups as diverse as historical Pentecostal denominations, the Catholic Renewal and the Third Wave Movement within mainline denominational churches. Engel and Norton discuss this in their insightful book, *What's Gone Wrong With the Harvest*:

> Church history also reveals some sobering lessons. When the Church retrenches into a static policy of resistance to change, it becomes a mere empty shell. The exterior trappings may appear adequate, but the interior vitality has long since expired. This, of course, is typical of a church in effectiveness crisis—going on, business as usual. But then a renaissance occurs—a breakthrough of the Holy Spirit, a new birth of relevance! All too often this new wine cannot be contained in the old wineskins and a new fellowship must be formed. At other times, the new life has infected the "empty" shell itself, reversed the effectiveness slide, and restored the body to its true function.[2]

THE POWER OF THE REMNANT

Spiritual revolution that grows out of reformation of doctrine and renewal of God's Spirit is implemented by a remnant of God's people. When God gets ready to do something big He chooses a remnant. God rarely does big things through the majority, as we can clearly see from the story of Gideon. God chose Gideon to lead His army against the

Midianites, Amalekites and "the sons of the east." The call to arms went out to Israel and approximately 32,000 volunteers gathered to fight against the army of 135,000 (Judges 7 and 8).

The two armies were close enough to engage in the Valley of Jezreel when God began to choose His remnant. God began His preparation by reducing the number of His army. If the war was won, Israel would say it was victorious because of their ability and numbers. Gideon was informed by God that the army was too large. 32,000 volunteers against 135,000 professional soldiers? "Lord, you've got to be kidding!" But Gideon sent God's word out to his volunteer army.

He said, "Any of you who are scared, who don't want to fight and want to go home, can leave." Gideon almost got trampled. 22,000 soldiers left for home post-haste. But God had still not found His remnant. Those 10,000 remaining soldiers were still too many and would claim they were responsible for victory. The remnant test was applied once again.

God said, "Watch the soldiers as they go down to drink. Those that lay their spears down at their sides and get down on all fours with their tails in the air, vulnerable, send home. Those that go down to the water, alert because they know they are in the battle zone, and who reach down with their cupped hands and drink with their spears in hand, keep."

How many were left? 300. Three hundred against 135,000. This was God's remnant. We must come to understand the power of the remnant. God was looking for a group that would depend upon Him, His might and His plan without any question.

God had to have a committed and obedient remnant because this was going to be God's kind of battle. That night God, through Gideon, told the soldiers about the battle plan and the weapons they were to use. What were the weapons? A pitcher, a candle and a trumpet. What would have happened if all of the 31,700 soldiers who had gone home had been given those instructions? When Gideon told them they were going to fight a night action, there would have been murmuring. When he told them about the weapons God had chosen for the battle, they would have certainly rebelled and broke ranks or gone to fight the enemy with conventional weapons. They would have suffered defeat.

What did the 300 do? They did not complain or rebel. They picked up those weapons and went to the battle. Why? They were such a small number by this time, it didn't matter what kind of weapons they used.

They couldn't defeat 135,000 soldiers with bazookas. A remnant, characteristically, is so small it must fight with God's plan and God's weapons at God's time with God's power. God's remnant is committed and obedient to doing things God's way.

God is calling out such a remnant today. You may be part of it. If you are, you will be required to exercise great faith and courage. Many will not respond to the call and measure up to the challenge. You will be part of the remnant, not because of your spirituality or ability, but because of your commitment to the battle and your willingness to fight the battle with God's weapons, God's plan, at God's time and with God's numbers.

RESTORATION OF DESIGN

The church is the hope for twenty-first century revolution. But what kind of church? What design? What structure? Can the church as we know it be used to fulfill the purpose God has for this age? Spiritual revolution in the twenty-first century cannot be effective apart from the reconstruction of a structural form through which pure doctrine, spiritual power and God's revelation can be expressed.

From time to time in history, the first three parts of this equation for revolution have come together. We have had the reformation of doctrine, revival of God's Spirit and God's remnant in place. But there was no spiritual revolution. Reformation took place but was poured back into the old wineskin. Movements of God's Spirit in history were isolated geographically and structurally. Remnants of God's people have come together periodically but without lasting results. These first three parts of the equation lacked a place from which spiritual revolution could explode. The final piece of the formula was lacking. No structure existed for molding the reformation, the revival, and the remnant into the spiritual body of Christ. Spiritual revolution must have a structure. That structure is the New Testament Two-Winged design of the church.

Unless there is a structural wineskin the wine of reformation, revival and remnant will gradually evaporate. This final element is coming into place in these last days before the second millennium. The New Testament cell design of the church promises to be the structure that will give the other elements the framework in which to become an explosive revolution. In the cell church movement, God is providing the structure through which the church can be the catalyst for spiritual revolution.

GOD IS IN THE BUSINESS OF REVOLUTION!

The Bible graphically proclaims that God spoke man's history into existence, and that history will end with a shout and a trumpet at Christ's second coming. History is not going in a circle as interpreted by Eastern thought, nor is it going backward as interpreted by the animist, nor is it going inward as interpreted by the New Age spiritualist, nor is it evolving upwards as interpreted by the scientist, nor is it going nowhere as claimed by the nihilist and atheist, nor is it spiraling downward toward the realm of darkness as claimed by the Satanist. But, history is moving forward toward a point in time predetermined by God, Who is actively involved in setting the course of history.

In his monumental history of the world, *The Story of Civilization*, Will Durant compares the influence of Caesar and Christ. He says of Jesus:

> The revolution he sought was a far deeper one, without which reforms could be only superficial and transitory. If he could cleanse the human heart of selfish desire, cruelty, and lust, utopia would come of itself, and all those institutions that rise out of human greed and violence, and the consequent need for law, would disappear. Since this would be the profoundest of all revolutions, beside which all others would be mere *coup d'etats* of class ousting class and exploiting in its turn, Christ was, in this spiritual sense the greatest revolutionist in history.[3]

Historian Edward Gibbon also appreciated what Christianity was as it compared to other revolutionary movements that had moved across history.

> While that great body [the Roman Empire] was invaded by open violence or undermined by slow decay, a pure and humble religion gently insinuated itself into the minds of men, grew up in silence and obscurity, derived new vigor from opposition, and finally erected the triumphant banner of the Cross on the ruins of the Capitol.[4]

THE CHURCH IS GOD'S INSTRUMENT

To most of us "holy history" refers either to what has happened in the past in church history or what will happen in the future when Christ returns. Seldom would we think of using the phrase holy history in reference to the present age. We are suspended in a state of second rate Christianity waiting for the important spiritual events of the second coming to take us out of this spiritually deprived age. It is a "circle the wagons" or "Scotty, beam me up!" perspective that echoes the cathedral mentality of the church. Surely God has not been caught unprepared for this time in history. God must have a way to reach out to the millions being born. Whatever God intends to do, He will do through His church. As Howard Snyder said in *Community of the King*:

> The Church is more than God's agent of evangelism or social change; it is, in submission to Christ, the agent of God's entire cosmic purpose. The Kingdom of God is coming, and to the extent that this coming of the Kingdom occurs in history before the return of Christ, God's plan is to be accomplished through the Church. . . .
> The Bible says the Church is nothing less than the body of Christ. It is the bride of Christ (Rev. 21:9), the flock of God (1 Pet. 5:2), the living temple of the Holy Spirit (Eph. 2:21-22). . . . If the Church is the body of Christ—the means for the head's action in the world—then the Church is an indispensable part of the gospel, and ecclesiology (theology dealing with the church) is inseparable from soteriology (theology dealing with salvation).[5]

It is imperative that the church perceive what God is doing and where He is going as He moves within history. Avery Willis describes history as "holy history" (heilsgeschichte) with the sweep of God's history underlying all that man calls history.

> God is not a mere spectator watching to see what men will do; he is an active participant in the redemption of lost humanity. . . . God is working in the lives of his children to send them into the harvest; he also is working in the people of the world to prepare them for the witness of his people. We must see his hand in the rising of the masses to seek a better life, in the restlessness of the nations. . . .

It is as if God wears a glove with each successive finger inscribed with the words: culture, politics, society, economics, and religion. God's hand is moving throughout all the affairs of men and of nations to produce a harvest.[6]

God's sweep of history goes from the creation of Adam and Eve all the way through Abraham and Moses, Gideon, the prophets, to the birth of Christ. Stephen was martyred because of his view of holy history. Read his remarkable sermon about God's holy history (see Acts 7). We possess in the New Testament the story of the early disciples. We know about Augustine and other church Fathers. We know the place of Luther and Wesley in God's holy history.

But where is the place of the twentieth century church? Where is our place in God's holy history? Is secular history so evil and corrupt that God can no longer use the church in His spiritual stream of history?

God's ability to make a difference in history has never depended upon the quality of His followers. It has always been God's sovereign will and power that has redeemed man's destructive history. Our place in God's history is the same as all those who have gone before us. We today are instruments of God's holy history through which He continues to redeem, renew and revolutionize.

No One Wears Shoes Here!

Two shoe companies wanted to open up a market in a new country. Each sent a salesman to evaluate the possibilities. Both salesmen discovered the same facts. No one wore shoes in that country. One salesman wired back to his company. "Cancel order. No one wears shoes here." The second salesman sent a wire back to his company. "Triple order. No one wears shoes here."

Like the story of the two shoe salesmen, Christians process the exact same facts but come up with diametrically opposing conclusions about the church in the world today.

Looking at the situation of the world we could conclude that we are living in a period of history dwarfed by what has happened in the past with the reformation. We are overwhelmed with what is happening today, and compelled to sit and wait for the end. But on the other hand, one with vision might say this period offers the greatest opportunity for harvest there has ever been. Can God not do a great thing today? Ralph

Neighbour has for years been the shoe salesman tripling the order. He has spoken of possibilities and opportunities:

> I am convinced that the traditional church worldwide is being slowly replaced by an act of God. Developments taking place today are as powerful as the upheaval in 1517 during the time of Martin Luther. One cannot say that Luther caused the first Reformation. He was only the tinder that lit the fire; the dead wood was ready to burn.
>
> Historians have examined the forces which came into play at that moment of time. The development of the printing press, the seething impatience with the greed of Rome, the growing disillusionment about philosophical systems, the emergence of scientific methods, all made that century a time of transition. The church was reformed by the hand of God to prepare it for the new world that was about to exist.
>
> The Catholicism of the Dark Ages was simply incompetent to cope with the new environment. The reformed church was a child of its time. It faced each new event with power from above. To be sure, it didn't come out of the old mold far enough—and the more conservative branches retained enough of the old ways to *burn at the stake* those who did go farther out.
>
> The styles of church life so appropriate for the Reformation period are now impotent. The church is impotent. It cannot reproduce unless it first physically fathers new children. I have roamed this earth since 1974, and the impotence is everywhere.
>
> It is time for the second Reformation. The people of earth have moved into a new era, one which never existed before in all the history of man. Change comes faster and faster, and the church becomes more and more irrelevant to cope with the changes.[7]

SMILE, SARA, SMILE!

How will the institutional church react to those who move in this Second Reformation? Confrontation along with amusement are two good possibilities. Leonardo Boff asks this question of the church concerning the stir caused by what he calls the modern "reinvention of the church." In light of these new expectations, the status quo smiles knowingly and skeptically at the enthusiasm and hope expressed.

Perhaps the institutional Church, with the experience and prudence of all older people, will smile upon hearing these reflections—like old Sara. She was sterile and believed it impossible for her to conceive. She smiles. Putting ourselves in Abraham's place, we hear God's question: "Why has Sara smiled? Is anything impossible for God?" (Gen. 18:14). Smile, Sara, because once sterile you have become fertile, you have become a new creation! Sara has already conceived. There, in Sara's womb, the signs of new life are already beginning to appear: a new Church is being born, in the dark recesses of humanity.[8]

So what will the wise old institutional church do in light of once again hearing about new cell church life? Hasn't change, renewal and even revolution been prophesied at other times in history when the church was still younger and of child bearing age? Now the Bride is old and the time is past! Play with Abraham's children by Hagar. Forget about new life out of the old body.

Smile at the thought of a new form growing out of the old. Chuckle at the thought of exuberant new life emerging out of that which is past age. Grin at the thought of the disruption of comfortable life with the cries and demands of new life. Snicker at the thought of having to reorder the old household in order to accommodate the new. But that smile of amusement and disbelief will turn to joyous laughter when the first stirrings are felt deep within the body of the mother. The amused smile will turn to joyous laughter. There will be pain in the birth, but the pain will issue forth in laughter because of the new life. So much joy that Abraham and Sara will even give this child the name Isaac, which means laughter.

In the beginning they probably smiled at Jesus, Peter, Paul, Luther, and Wesley. Why make a big deal of these things? You will come around eventually and see that the organ for birth is too old and rigid and dry. Adopt! Get a cute pet. Find programs that are the children of others and play with them. Find surrogates. Be satisfied in your old age. Play with other people's children, and know that once old you will not conceive something new.

Yes, the status quo smiles when the birth of new church revolutions are whispered. Boff gives the following warning to those who smile their knowing smile in the face of God's revolution:

This is still just the beginning, still in process. It is not an accomplished reality. Pastors and theologians, take warning! Respect this new way that is appearing on the horizon. Do not seek at once to box this phenomenon within theological-pastoral categories distilled from other contexts and other ecclesial experiences. Instead, assume the attitude of those who would see, understand, and learn.[9]

END NOTES

Introduction
1. T. S. Kuhn, *The Copernican Revolution* (Cambridge, Mass., 1957), 138, quoted in Thomas S. Kuhn, *The Structure of Scientific Revolutions* (Chicago: University of Chicago Press, 1962), 83.

Section I
Elton Trueblood, *Your Other Vocation* (New York: Harper and Brothers, 1952), 32.

Chapter One
1. Christian Smith, "Tub Drains, Planets, & Mountain Bikes: On the Need for an Ecclesiological Paradigm Shift," *Voices Newsletter,* Number 1, 1.
2. Smith *Voices Newsletter*, Number 1, 1.
3. Stephen R. Covey, Principle-Centered Leadership (New York: Simon and Schuster, 1991), 67.
4. Herb Miller, ed., "Letter to President Jackson," *Net Results Magazine,* March 1991.
5. Edward de Bono, *Lateral Thinking* (New York: Harper & Row, 1970), 13-14.
6. Joel A. Barker, *Discovering the Future* (Lake Elmo, MN: I. L. I. Press, 1989), 60.

Chapter Two
"Perhaps the church . . ." Elton Trueblood, *Yoke of Christ* (New York: Harper and Brothers, 1958), 115.
1. Ralph W. Neighbour Jr., "Welcome to the Cell Church!," *Cell Church Magazine*, August 1994, 5.
2. Quoted in Robert Banks, *The Home Church* (Sutherland, Australia: Albatross Books, 1986), 70.

Chapter Three
"One of the tragedies . . ." Samuel Miller, "The Evaluation of Religion," Saturday Review, 14 November 1959, 70, quoted in Robert A. Raines, *New Life in the Church* (New York: Harper & Row, 1961), 141.
1. Raines, *New Life in the Church*, 141.
2. H. S. Vigeveno, *Jesus The Revolutionary* (Glendale, CA: G/L

Publications: 1966), 3.
3. Elton Trueblood, *The Company of the Committed* (New York: Harper & Brothers, 1961), 26.
4. Fred W. Waterman, "Those Fabulous Fakes," *Hemispheres Magazine*, (July 1994) : 78, 80.
5. Waterman, *Hemispheres Magazine* (July 1994) : 77.
6. Gerald Kennedy, *The Parables* (New York: Harper & Row, 1960), 56.
7. Juan Carlos Ortiz, *Disciple* (Altamonte Springs, FL: Creation House, 1975), 84.
8. Johann Baptist Metz, Faith In History and Society, quoted in Bernard J. Lee and Michael A. Cowan, *Dangerous Memories* (Kansas City, MO: Sheed and Ward, 1986), iv.

Chapter Four

"The basic trouble . . ." Trueblood, *The Company of the Committed*, 10.
1. H.G. Bosch, "He Left No Vacancy," Our Daily Bread, May 1974, quoted in James F. Engel and H. Wilbert Norton, *What's Gone Wrong With The Harvest?* (Grand Rapids: MI Zondervan Publishing House, 1975), 156.
2. Eutychus, "Fear of Flying," *Christianity Today,* 20 June 1994, 6.
3. Lyle E. Schaller, *The Change Agent* (Nashville, TN: Abingdon Press, 1972), 97.
4. Elton Trueblood, *The Validity of the Christian Mission* (New York: Harper & Row, 1972), 93.
5. John R. Mott, Liberating the Lay Forces of Christianity (New York: The Macmillian Company, 1932), 84, quoted in Trueblood, *Your Other Vocation*, 49.

Chapter Five

"This one lifetime . . ." Alvin Toffler, Future Shock (New York: Random House, 1970), 15, quoted in Os Guinness, *the Dust of Death* (Downers Grove, IL: InterVarsity Press, 1973), 47.
1. Michael Barone, "Slouching toward dystopia," *U. S. News and World Report*, 20 December 1993, 34.
2. "Warn the Storks," *Houston Chronicle: Newsmaker Column,* 18 May 1992, 2A.
3. David B. Barrett, *World Class Cities and World Class Evangelism* (Birmingham, AL: New Hope, 1986), 21.
4. David B. Barrett, *World Class Cities and World Class Evangelism,* 10.

Chapter Six
"Speed is useful . . ." Joel A. Barker, *Paradigm*, 208.
1. Trueblood, *The Company of the Committed*, 6.
2. E. Stanley Jones, *The Reconstruction of the Church—On What Pattern?* (Nashville: Abingdon, 1970), 18.
3. Jones, *The Reconstruction of the Church—On What Pattern?*, 18.
4. Ralph W. Neighbour Jr., The Shepherd's Guidebook, Revised Edition (Houston: TOUCH Publications, 1994), 156.
5. Banks, *The Home Church*, p. 52.
6. Robert Wuthnow, "How Small Groups Are Transforming Our Lives," *Christianity Today* 38 (7 February 1994) : 21.
7. Warren Bird, "The Great Small-Group Takeover," Christianity Today 38 (7 February 1994) : 26

Chapter Seven
"It is neither . . ." Trueblood, *Yoke of Christ*, 113.
1. Kuhn, *The Structure of Scientific Revolutions,* 153.
2. Kuhn, *The Structure of Scientific Revolutions,* 18.
3. Donald A. McGavran, *Understanding Church Growth* (Grand Rapids MI: Wm B. Eerdmans, 1970), 192.
4. Earnest Loosley, *When The Church Was Young* (Auburn, ME: Christian Books Publishing House, 1935), 11.
5. Howard A. Snyder, *The Problem of Wineskins* (Peabody, MA: Hendrickson Publishers, 1988), 78-9.
6. Howard A. Snyder, *Signs of the Spirit* (Grand Rapids, MI: Zondervan, 1989), 260.

Chapter Eight
1. J. I . Packer, *Knowing God* (London: Hodder & Stoughton, 1973), 88.
2. C. S. Lewis, *The Problem of Pain* (New York: The Macmillan Company, 1962), 41.
3. Howard A. Snyder, *The Problem of Wineskins* (Peabody, MA: Hendrickson Publishers, 1988), 97.
4. David and Pat Alexander, eds. *The Lion Handbook of the Bible*, 2nd ed., (Herts, England: Lion Publishing, 1983), s.v. "The Names of God," by Alec Motyer, 157.

Chapter Nine
"in Christ . . ." E. Y. Mullins, *The Christian Religion in Its Doctrinal*

Expression (Nashville, TN: Broadman Press, 1945), 173.

1. Francis A. Schaeffer, *True Spirituality* (Wheaton, IL: Tyndale House Publishers, 1971), 72.

2. Schaeffer, *True Spirituality*, 172.

3. Earnest Loosely, *When the Church Was Young* (Auburn, ME: Christian Books Publishing House, 1935), 79.

4. Ray Stedman, Body Life (Glendale, CA: Regal Books, 1972), 130.

5. Schaeffer, *The Church at the End of the 20th Century,* 66.

Chapter Ten

"There is to be . . ." Schaeffer, *The Church at the End of the 20th Century,* 56.

1. Snyder, *Community of the King*, 147.

2. Elton Trueblood, *The Incendiary Fellowship* (New York: Harper & Row, 1967), 89.

3. Stedman, *Body Life*, 108.

4. F. F. Bruce, *The Spreading Flame* (Grand Rapids, MI: Wm. B. Eerdmans Publishing Company, 1958), 15.

5. Michael Green, *Evangelism in the Early Church* (Grand Rapids, MI: Wm. B. Eerdman's Publishing Company, 1970), 208.

6. John N. Vaughan, *The Large Church* (Grand Rapids, MI: Baker Book House, 1985), .41.

7. William Barclay, *The Lord's Supper* (London: SCM, 1967), 101-104, quoted in Banks, *The Home Church*, 59.

Chapter Eleven

"The Reformation . . ." William R. Estep, *The Anabaptist Storm* (Grand Rapids, MI: Wm. B. Eerdmans, 1975), p.182.

1. Martin Luther, *Luther's Works*, vol. 53, Preface to The German Mass and Order of Service, gen. ed. Helmut T. Lehmann, trans. Paul Zeller Strodach (Philadelphia: Fortress Press, 1965), 63-64.

2. D. M. Lloyd Jones, "Ecclesiola in Ecclesia," Approaches to the Reformation of the Church, (Papers from the Puritan and Reformed Studies Conference), 1965, pp. 60-61.

3. Kenneth J. Derksen, "The Collegium Pietatis as a Model for Home Bible Study Groups," *Crux* XXII no. 4 (December 1986): 20, quoted in Doyle L. Young, *New Life For Your Church* (Grand Rapids, MI: Baker Book House, 1989), 107.

4. Derksen, "The Collegium Pietatis," 21, quoted in Young, *New Life For*

Your Church 108-9.

5. Howard A. Snyder, *The Radical Wesley and Patterns of Church Renewal* (Downers Grove, IL: Inter-Varsity Press, 1980), 54-55.

6. John Wesley, *Wesley's Works* vol. 8 (London, Wesleyan-Methodist Book-Room), 251

7. *Wesley's Works* vol. 2, 482

8. *Wesley's Letters* vol. 7, 154.

9. R. W. Stott, *One People: Laymen and Clergy in God's Church* (Downers Grove, IL: Inter-Varsity Press paperback), p. 88, quoted in Stedman, *Body Life*, 112.

10. C. Kirk Hadaway, Stuart A. Wright and Francis M. DuBose, *Home Cell Groups and House Churches* (Nashville: Broadman Press, 1987), 233.

Chapter Twelve

"There must be . . ." Schaeffer, *True Spirituality,* 171.

1. Dr. Wallace, "Who's Afraid of the Holy Spirit," *Christianity Today* 12 September 1994, 35.

2. Rodman Williams, *Renewal Theology Vol. 1* (Grand Rapids, MI: Zondervan, 1988), 146.

3. Schaeffer, *True Spirituality*, 63.

4. Schaeffer, *True Spirituality*, 63.

5. "Baby Boomer Exodus from Church Noted," *Houston Chronicle* June 5, 1992, 12A.

6. Schaeffer, *The Church at the End of the 20th Century*, 71, 72.

7. Engel and Norton, *What's Gone Wrong With The Harvest?*, 136.

Chapter Thirteen

"If God . . ." Trueblood, *Company of the Committed*, 113.

1. Raines, *New Life in the Church*, 103.

Chapter Fourteen

"The system . . ." Quoted in Michael E. Gerber, *The E Myth: Why Most Small Businesses Don't Work and What to Do About It* (New York: HarperCollins, 1986): 109.

1. Peter R. Scholtes, *The Team Handbook: How to Use Teams to Improve Quality* (Madison, WI: Joiner Associates Inc., 1988): 2-8.

2. Lyle E. Schaller, *The Change Agent: The Strategy of Innovative Leadership* (Nashville: Abingdon, 1972): 175.

3. Gerber, *The E-Myth,* 60.
4. Gerber, *The E-Myth,* 55.
5. Gerber, *The E-Myth,* 60, 61.
6. Gerber, *The E-Myth,* 141.
7. James F. Hind, *The Heart and Soul of Effective Management: A Christian Approach to Managing and Motivating People*, quoted in *Life* (December 1994): 79.
8. Schaller, *The Change Agent,* 89.
9. Christopher Sower and others, *Community Involvement*, (Glencoe: Free Press 1958), 306-314, quoted in Schaller, *The Change Agent,* 89.

Chapter Fifteen
"Every activity . . ." W. Edwards Deming, *Out of Crisis* (Cambridge: Massachusetts Institute of Technology Center for Advanced Engineering Study, 1986), 87.
1. *Webster's New World Dictionary*, (1990).
2. Raines, *New Life in the Church*, 78.

Chapter Sixteen
"The Prototype . . ." Gerber, *The E-Myth*, 54.
1. W. Jack Duncan and Joseph G. Van Metre, "The Gospel According to Deming. Is It Really New?" *Business Horizons*, July-Aug. 1990, 5.
2. Gerber, *The E-Myth*, 54.
3. Deming, *Out of Crisis*, 128-9.

Chapter Seventeen
"The Prototype . . ." Gerber, *The E-Myth*, 55.
1. Coleman, *The Master Plan of Evangelism* (Old Tappen, NJ: Revell Co., 1963), 21.
2. Ralph W. Neighbour Jr., *Where Do We Go From Here? A Guidebook for the Cell Group Church* (Houston: TOUCH Publications, 1990), 202.
3. Stedman, *Body Life*, 114.
4. E. Stanley Jones, *The Way* (New York: Abingdon-Codesbury Press, 1946), 272.

Chapter Eighteen
"One must decide . . ." Coleman, *The Master Plan of Evangelism*, 37.
1. Coleman, *The Master Plan of Evangelism*, 109.
2. Coleman, *The Master Plan of Evangelism*, 31-32.

3. Paul M. Zehr and Jim Egli, *Alternative Models of Mennonite Pastoral Formation* (Elkhart, IN: Institute of Mennonite Studies, 1992), 43.
4. Coleman, *The Master Plan of Evangelism,* 46.
5. Coleman, *The Master Plan of Evangelism,* 26.
6. Deming, *Out of Crisis*, 129.

Chapter Nineteen
"But if a paradigm . . ." Kuhn, *The Structure of Scientific Revolutions*, 158.
1. Schaller, *The Change Agent,* 104-109.
2. Dietrich Bonhoeffer, *Life Together* (San Francisco: Harper and Row, 1954), 27-28.

Chapter Twenty
"The small group . . ." Snyder, *The Problem of Wineskins*, 144.
1. Yonggi Cho with Harold Hostetler, *Successful Home Cell Groups* (South Plainfield, NJ: Bridge Publishing, 1981), 21-24.
2. Karen Hurston, *Growing the World's Largest Church* (Springfield, MO: Gospel Publishing House, 1994), 86.

Chapter Twenty-One
"Much of the . . ." Trueblood, *The Incendiary Fellowship*, 107.
1. John Stott, *The Spirit, the Church and the World: The Message of Acts* (Downers Grove, IL: InterVarsity Press, 1990), 59.
2. Stott, *The Spirit, the Church and the World*, 59.
3. *The World Book Dictionary*, 1978 ed.
4. Stott, *The Spirit, the Church and the World,* 89.
5. Jess Moody, *A Drink at Joel's' Place* (Waco, TX: Word, 1967), 22, 17, quoted in Snyder, *The Problem of Wineskins*, 105.
6. Lee and Cowan, *Dangerous Memories*, 35.
7. Stedman, *Body Life*, 15.
8. Stedman, *Body Life*, 37-38.
9. W.O. Carver, Forward to *What is the Church?* by Duke McCall (Nashville: Broadman Press, 1958), 3.
10. W. O. Carver, *The Glory of God in the Christian Calling* (Nashville: Broadman Press, 1949), 42, quoted in Charles L. Chaney, *Church Planting at the End of the Twentieth Century* (Wheaton, IL: Tyndale, 1982), 22.
11. Stedman, *Body Life*, 94.

12. C. H. Dodd, *The Founder of Christianity* (New York: The MacMillan Co., 1970), 171-172.

Chapter Twenty-Two
1. Peter R. Scholtes, *The Team Handbook*, 1/22.
2. C. Peter Wagner, *Church Planting for a Greater Harvest* (Ventura, CA: Regal Books, 1990), 119.
3. George Barna, *The Power of Vision* (Ventura, CA: Regal Books, 1992), 28-41.
4. Oswald Chamber, *My Utmost for His Highest* (New York: Dodd, Mead and Co., 1961), 188, 71.
5. Barna, *The Power of Vision*, 29.
6. Trueblood, *The Company of the Committed*, 22-23.
7. *Othello* 2.3.376
8. Gene Edwards, *A Tale of Three Kings* (Wheaton, IL: Tyndale House, 1992), 47-48.
9. Snyder, *Signs of the Spirit* (Grand Rapids, MI: Zondervan 1989), 290.
10. Coleman, *The Master Plan of Evangelism*, 75.

Conclusion
"It is the depravity . . ." E. Stanley Jones, *The Reconstruction of the Church-On What Pattern?* (Nashville, TN: Abingdon Press, 1970), 8.
1. Francis A. Schaeffer, *Death in the City* (Chicago, IL: Inter-Varsity Press, 1969), 9.
2. Engel and Norton, *What's Gone Wrong With The Harvest?*, 136.
3. Quoted in Stedman, *Body Life*, 11
4. Quoted in Stedman, *Body Life,* 18.
5. Howard A. Snyder, *The Community of the King* (Downers Grove, IL: Inter-varsity Press, 1977), 55.
6. Avery Willis Jr., *Biblical Basis of Missions* (Nashville, TN: Convention Press, 1979), 154.
7. Neighbour, *Where Do We Go From Here?*, 6.
8. Leonardo Boff, *Church: Charism and Power* (New York: Crossroad Publishing Company, 1981), 64.
9. Leonardo Boff, "ecclesiogenesis," *Voices Newsletter*, July 1986, 14.

OTHER CELL CHURCH RESOURCES

Where Do We Go From Here? **By Ralph W. Neighbour Jr.**
"This may be the second-most important book you will ever read."
Dive head-first into the vision for the cell-based church. Learn the
overall structure and strategy of the cell church from a true pioneer.
Find keys to successful basic Christian communities. Catch a vision
for your church's future.

Shepherd's Guidebook **By Ralph W. Neighbour Jr.**
Dr. Neighbour draws from over 25 years of small group experience
to paint the life of a cell group. What does it take to lead a cell group?
Who makes up a cell? How large should they be and how do they
grow? What do you do in a weekly meeting? Find answers to these
questions and more and become an equipped cell leader. Includes 12
sample cell meeting agendas and forms to launch your journey.

Life In His Body: A Simple Guide to Active Cell Life **By Dr. David
Finnell**
Key leaders and members must catch a personal vision for cell
involvement. *Life in His Body* explains the cell vision in simple
language and challenges the reader to personally commit to the essential elements of a successful cell church—prayer, community,
evangelism, and leadership. Communicate the vision clearly to others
with *Life in His Body*.

House to House **By Larry Kreider**
"This is the story of how a small band of young people dared to live
by these (cell group) principles and became a mighty army of God.
Dare we do the same?"—Floyd McClung Jr., Author and Speaker.
Learn from the experience of 15 years and 2000 members in cell
groups.

The TOUCH Equipping Track for Cell Members

TOUCH's vision is that every member of the Body of Christ be equipped to do the work of ministry. Though discipleship is inherently a spiritual thing, in order for Christians to be equipped there must be certain "spiritual stations" along the journey to maturity. Essentially, the equipping track seeks to balance the spiritual and the natural in the discipleship process. Each station is a handle both new and older Christians can grip as they grow spiritually and move along their personal "track." The equipping track is not meant to be a "magic disciple-machine" or a quick formula, but a model for intentional teaching, training, and sending—a model that has been tested and re-tested all over the world. Use it as a model for your equipping track in your unique situation.

Welcome to Your Changed Life begins the journey with a clarification of the life changing decision the new Christian has made. *The Journey Guide* gives the new cell member a simple understanding of where he is on his journey, and the commitment the cell has made to help him grow in the Lord. *The Arrival Kit* brings foundational biblical principles to light, and includes a section especially for the sponsor. *The Sponsor's Guidebook* follows as station four. Cell members will find more spiritual growth comes through serving others as a sponsor, and this station tests their value system as they commit to discipling another. It gives practical handles for edifying another Christian. *The Touching Hearts Guidebook* takes the cell member out of the cell and into the lives of easy-to-reach unbelievers, teaching simple principles to bring them to Christ. Station six, *The Opening Hearts Trilogy* launches "share groups" to penetrate the world of the hard-core unbeliever. The last station, a parallel track entitled *Cover The Bible*, gives cell members a fascinating look at the entire Bible in a year. Listening to cassettes recorded in the pastor's voice, they will receive a bible college level survey of the Scriptures.

Cell Church Magazine

This quarterly resource for cell members and leadership provides current insights on this movement that is spreading across the world. Hear the testimonies of pastors who are on the road of cell church life. Gain practical information that is essential to life in the structure. Each issue contains a cell leader "toolkit" filled with problem solving techniques, testimonies of other cell leaders and ways to foster community, discipleship and evangelism. Expect to find in each issue:

• Skill training for leaders
• Vision casting for members
• New resources and conferences
• Transitioning tools
• Help with children and youth cells
• Practical ideas for cell life
• A pulse on the second reformation

Everyone benefits. Include all your leadership through a bulk subscription and watch them grow!

Call TOUCH Outreach Ministries at 1-800-735-5865 if in the United States and 281-497-7901 if calling outside the U.S. for a free catalog on these and other TOUCH Publications.